START WITH QUESTIONS

START WITH QUESTIONS

THE CLASSROOM AS DESIGN STUDIO

KAREN BRENNAN AND SARAH BLUM-SMITH

Foreword by MITCHEL RESNICK

THE MIT PRESS   CAMBRIDGE, MASSACHUSETTS   LONDON, ENGLAND

The MIT Press
Massachusetts Institute of Technology
77 Massachusetts Avenue
Cambridge, MA 02139
mitpress.mit.edu

The MIT Press would like to thank the anonymous peer reviewers who provided comments on drafts of this book. The generous work of academic experts is essential for establishing the authority and quality of our publications. We acknowledge with gratitude the contributions of these otherwise uncredited readers.

This book was set in Stone Serif and AvenirLT std Medium by Westchester Publishing Services. Printed and bound in the United States of America.

Excerpts from *Teaching as a Subversive Activity* by Neil Postman and Charles Weingartner, used by permission from Penguin Random House.

Library of Congress Cataloging-in-Publication Data is available.

ISBN: 978-0-262-05146-0

10 9 8 7 6 5 4 3 2

EU Authorised Representative: Easy Access System Europe, Mustamäe tee 50, 10621 Tallinn, Estonia | Email: gpsr.requests@easproject.com

CONTENTS

FOREWORD

Mitchel Resnick

Almost everyone agrees on the need to improve education and learning. But there are many different perspectives on how to do it.

People with an engineering background often look for ways to improve student performance by optimizing the efficiency of the learning process. People with a business background often propose market-based approaches to education, suggesting ways to incentivize teachers and learners. People with a scientific background often focus on how advances in the understanding of the brain will lead to improvements in education and learning.

In this important new book, Karen Brennan and Sarah Blum-Smith offer a much-needed alternative to these approaches. Drawing on ideas from the fields of architecture and design, they invite teachers to view the classroom as a design studio, providing students with opportunities to create their own projects, experiment with new ideas, learn from others, and reflect on their experiences.

This studio approach is a radical departure from what happens in most of today's schools, where the focus is often on efficiently delivering instruction to prepare students for standardized exams. The authors make a compelling case for change, highlighting how the studio approach can provide a motivating context for students to develop a greater confidence in themselves as self-directed learners, experience the joys of learning, and make deeper and more meaningful connections to important domains of knowledge.

What makes the book so compelling is the way it integrates practice and theory. At the core of the book are forty stories from K–12 classrooms, providing concrete examples of how teachers are putting the studio approach into practice. Each story is paired with a theory-based analysis through the lens of a particular educational theorist, including Maria Montessori, John Dewey, Paulo Freire, bell hooks, Seymour Papert, Carol Dweck, and many others from across the past two hundred years.

The authors succeed in making educational theory very accessible, since theoretical ideas are always grounded in real-world classroom practice—and presented in a crisply clear writing style (much more accessible than the texts of many of the original theorists!). In each story, quotes from the classroom teacher are mixed with quotes from the selected theorist. Theory is presented in bite-size chunks, making it easily digestible but without losing any of its rich flavor.

A major challenge in implementing the studio approach (and a major theme throughout the book) is how to support students as self-directed learners. Too often, people imagine education as a tension between two extremes: either teachers dictate what students do, or they let students do whatever they want. The authors acknowledge "the perceived contradiction between self-direction and support" but argue that the two can be "mutually reinforcing rather than in tension." They explain: "There is a delicate and elusive balance between offering learners the freedom to pursue their own interests and providing enough support for learners to be successful. . . . Ultimately, supporting self-direction in the K–12 classroom involves intentional, thoughtful work on the part of the teacher, who navigates the nebulous space between total lack of support and total control over the learner."

The forty stories at the core of the book can be viewed as an extended exploration of how teachers can support students in developing as self-directed learners. As the authors write: "These teachers want the students in their classrooms to trust in themselves, as people with ideas, as people who can figure things out. They want their students to have an increased sense of reliance on themselves—for deciding what is important, for knowing how to do things, for judging what works and what does not."

Each of the book's forty stories starts with a question posed by the teacher featured in the story, such as "What are you interested in?" or "What are you trying to do?" or "What would you have done if you had more time?" Of course, teachers in traditional classrooms ask questions too, but they usually know the answer to the questions they ask, and they want the students to figure it out. The questions that teachers pose in studio-based classrooms are quite different, more genuine, without a "right" answer. The questions are designed to spark students' imaginations and engage them in new explorations.

With this book, in a recursive twist, Karen Brennan and Sarah Blum-Smith are also trying to do something similar for teachers, aiming to spark their imaginations and engage them in new explorations. Just as the book encourages teachers to support their students in becoming self-directed creators and learners, the book's authors also want teachers to become self-directed creators and learners themselves. Before sharing the forty stories, the authors write: "We encourage you to engage with this collection in whatever way feels meaningful to you. You may want to read the collection from start to finish. Or you may want to just jump in somewhere, with a question that provokes your curiosity, a classroom context that seems similar to your own, or a theorist who is calling to you." And directly after sharing the stories, they write: "We invite you to make a list of ideas, themes, or questions in response to the prompt: *What did you see?*"

As you read this book, I encourage you to follow the authors' suggestions and invitations. In today's complex world, as the pace of change continues to accelerate, it's more important than ever for teachers and students to develop as self-directed creators and learners. Exploring the ideas and stories in this book is a great place to start.

I

FOUNDATIONS

WHAT ARE THE MOST IMPORTANT QUESTIONS?

In the blank space below (or another suitable place), write down the most important questions you have been asked as a learner. Your learning may have happened at an earlier time in your life, or more recently. Your learning may have happened in a school classroom, or in another venue. List as many of these questions as you can recall, recording any memories or ideas that surface. If it is helpful to have another constraint, set a ten-minute timer for yourself.

In their 1971 book *Teaching as a Subversive Activity*,[1] Neil Postman and Charles Weingartner argued that what we ask learners to *do* is what they *learn*—and that there is often misalignment between what educators ask their students to do and what educators claim to value. They identified teachers' questions as a powerful example of this misalignment, suggesting that students too often encounter "what might technically be called 'convergent questions,' but which might more simply be called 'Guess what I'm thinking' questions."[2] These are questions that have right answers, questions that don't invite further exploration. They close off inquiry and dreaming, rather than open up possibilities. These questions communicate to learners that they aren't capable or deserving of weightier work, of thinking and creation beyond the boundaries the questions have imposed. What did you notice in the list of questions you generated from your own experience? What did those questions make possible for you as a learner?

Rather than offering a fixed or ideal set of questions to ask learners, Postman and Weingartner offered a set of principles for the questions we should ask and be asked. Unsurprisingly, they expressed those principles as questions:

- Will your questions increase the learner's will as well as [their] capacity to learn?
- Will they help to give [the learner] a sense of joy in learning?
- Will they help to provide the learner with confidence in [their] ability to learn?
- In order to get answers, will the learner be required to make inquiries? (Ask further questions, clarify terms, make observations, classify data, etc.?)
- Does each question allow for alternative answers (which implies alternative modes of inquiry)?
- Will the process of answering the questions tend to stress the uniqueness of the learner?
- Would the questions produce different answers if asked at different stages of the learner's development?
- Will the answers help the learner to sense and understand the universals in the human condition and so enhance [their] ability to draw closer to other people?[3]

As I thought about this exercise in the context of my own life, I identified three questions that I have been asked as a learner and that embody these principles. These three questions, and my responses to them, serve as the foundation and motivation for this book: *What are you excited about? What are you inspired to share with others? What do you need to create?*

WHAT ARE YOU EXCITED ABOUT?

I completed my PhD in 2012 at the MIT Media Lab, as a member of the Lifelong Kindergarten research group directed by Mitch Resnick. My very first meeting with Mitch as a doctoral student was, in hindsight, an excellent preview of what my experiences would be like as a learner in this new environment. After sharing a little about the structure and workings of his research group, Mitch asked me, "What are you excited about?" I remember my mind racing in the pause that followed. *Was I already supposed to know what sorts of projects I was going to work on? Should I have developed a plan?* After a moment or two of silence, I confessed that I wasn't sure. Mitch kindly reassured me that this wasn't a question for this moment, but rather a question that I should use to guide my work during my time at the Lab. He encouraged me to explore expansively, to work with many different people on many different projects, and to never lose that thread of personal excitement, interest, and passion.

Throughout my time at the Lab, I was invited to dream and to create in a way that I hadn't ever experienced before, to work on projects and explore ideas that mattered to me and were exciting to me. I was both deeply trusted to be self-directed in my learning and deeply supported. I was also given new language and new theory for understanding this approach to learning that centers learning through creating, that values connecting to personal interests, that encourages interacting with community, and that invites thinking about one's own thinking.

The name for this approach to learning is *constructionism*. Developed by Mitch's mentor Seymour Papert as an extension of Jean Piaget's constructivism, constructionism values learners' sense of agency and capacity for self-direction, appreciates the power of learning in community with supportive others (such as peers, facilitators, and teachers), and underscores the importance of bringing one's ideas into the world, in whatever form those ideas might invite, from poems, to performances, to computer programs.[4] The special confluence of being introduced to the language of constructionism while simultaneously experiencing it illuminated not only the focus of my research at the time, but also elements of my own learning history. Looking back on a lifetime of learning, I could easily see how my most important learning experiences, in and out of school, across my life, have had the key qualities of a constructionist approach.

At the Media Lab, I saw constructionism in action in the research projects I was working on, most notably my involvement in the development of Scratch, a programming environment and online community that has grown enormously since its release in 2007. I joined Mitch's group just as Scratch was initially launched. I don't think any of us anticipated how much the community would grow and how it would become a space for so many young people to engage in self-directed learning within a community of creators.

My observations and interactions with young creators in the Scratch community, as well as my own learning experiences as a graduate student, underscored that self-direction doesn't happen despite support, but because of it. With the right structures, supports, and scaffolds, we are better positioned to bring our wonderful, powerful, beautiful ideas into the world. With too little support or too much support or the wrong support, our ideas get lost or suffocated. Understanding this balance between self-direction and support in learning environments has been an ongoing obsession of mine since my time at the Media Lab.

WHAT ARE YOU INSPIRED TO SHARE WITH OTHERS?

After Lifelong Kindergarten, I started as a faculty member at the Harvard Graduate School of Education (HGSE). As I was getting oriented, learning about the culture at Harvard, I had a meeting with Matt Miller, the Assistant Dean for Academic Affairs at that time, to discuss what I would teach. I expected that, like my colleagues recently hired at other institutions, I would be assigned courses to teach. So I was surprised when Matt explained that HGSE followed a "signature course" model, one in which

I would get to decide what I would teach. After explaining the model, Matt, with his characteristic enthusiasm, asked me, "What are you inspired to share with others?"

I knew that I wanted to create a learning experience that captured some of the beauty and joy I had experienced as a graduate student. Inspired by a course that Mitch taught, and that Seymour Papert taught before him, I decided to teach a course about designing learning experiences. The course explores constructionism as an approach to learning design and is itself organized as a constructionist learning experience, with students developing and pursuing self-directed projects over the thirteen weeks of the term. With the help of many wonderful collaborators, I've been able to share this course, full of inspiring ideas that I love so much, with more than fifteen hundred students.

One might imagine that a class about learning through creating in community would take place in a makerspace-like environment, full of flexible seating, tables to work at and share from, and a variety of materials and tools. Instead, the class has typically been scheduled in a large lecture hall. There are many ways that we have adapted to this constraint over the years, such as occupying adjacent hallways and outdoor spaces or rolling in carts of materials for creating and making. More essential than these physical adaptations, however, is how we engage our collective thinking about the space.

And so I begin each term by inviting everyone into a thought experiment. I ask them to imagine that we are not in a lecture hall. I suggest that we will collectively transform the room and all that it suggests about the didacticism assumed in education—trading lecture for conversation, note-taking for a wider range of creative documentation, and passivity for collective construction.

Through a series of images projected on a large screen at the front of the room, I offer an alternative vision of the space. Our lecture hall might sometimes feel like a laboratory, full of experimentation and inquiry. At other times it might feel like a sandbox, messy and fluid. Sometimes it might feel like an orchestra pit, collaborative and synchronous. Or it might evoke an art gallery, polished and presentation oriented. There might be moments when the lecture hall feels like a street party, playful and boisterous.

I offer these images to my students as metaphors for what the experience of learning in this classroom will feel like, as a way of disrupting some of the expectations that we all carry with us based on prior experiences and understandings. Metaphors are invitations to imagine, helping us articulate possibilities and aspirations. When you think about what classrooms are and what they could be, what metaphors are most inspiring to you?

A metaphor that I have been finding especially generative in my research and teaching is that of the *design studio*. While the idea of constructionism can feel vague (or too easily confused with constructivism) when used to describe a classroom that embodies its qualities, I have found design studio to be a satisfying and evocative phrase for encapsulating what I see and hear and feel in a constructionist classroom.

The design studio has been central to architecture education, with learning-by-doing serving as its signature pedagogy.[5] Imagining the classroom as design studio makes possible new conceptions of the activities, relationships, and responsibilities that characterize that learning environment. This metaphor suggests we are working on projects, in self-directed and reflective ways, alongside others who are also working on things that matter to them. It suggests an honoring of the expertise and support offered by teachers, support that focuses on helping learners bring their own ideas into being.

The classroom as design studio serves as the central metaphor of this book; it takes the abstract idealism of constructionism as a theory, with self-direction as one of its core commitments, and gives it shape and form. To call this a metaphor is to offer the design studio as suggestive rather than prescriptive, as an image that can clarify values and generate thinking rather than a template to follow. Despite the limitations of any metaphorical comparison, I hope the image of the design studio will be helpful to you, as it has been helpful to me.

WHAT DO YOU NEED TO CREATE?

Although I am grateful for my experiences at MIT and the learning I've observed in the Scratch online community and my courses at Harvard, I acknowledge that these are incredibly precious contexts. Our thinking about what is valuable and meaningful in education cannot be constrained to rarified environments. K–12 schools should be places where all learners have access to these types of learning experiences: environments where they can work on projects and explore ideas that feel important to them, where their voices and impulses are honored, and where they have access to peers and teachers who support them on their learning journeys. For reasons too many to name here, this too often is not the case in K–12 classrooms today. The challenges endemic to public education make it hard and dampen our ability to imagine what could be.

But there *are* teachers who have been able to navigate this complexity. In K–12 classrooms where this kind of self-directed learning is already happening, what does it look like? What is making it possible?

These questions have motivated my work for the past eighteen years. I have been especially interested in the relationship between self-direction and support in the context of K–12 schools and the special role that teachers play in the design of learning experiences. From my research, I feel confident in asserting that *yes*, self-directed learning is possible in K–12 classrooms—and this learning is happening in classrooms around the United States and around the world every day.

To be responsive to my students at Harvard who have been eager to know what this approach could look like in practice, and to honor the inspiring educators who are doing this work in classrooms every day, I wanted to create something that could support our collective pedagogical imaginations. But I wasn't entirely sure what it could be.

Although the pandemic that shut the world down in early 2020 was an incredible hardship for so many people, in so many ways, I am grateful that those unfortunate circumstances led to an unexpected collaborative opportunity. One of my phenomenal graduate students, Sarah Blum-Smith, had just completed her doctoral degree. Her dream was to return to the K–12 classroom, but the timing of her return was delayed by the pandemic.

I asked Sarah if she might be interested in staying at HGSE as a postdoctoral scholar, an opportunity to build on our many years of collaborative work together, studying teachers and their learning, engaging in regular and joyful reading of educational theory and philosophy. It was an incredible gift that she said yes, and I am so grateful that we were able to work together for three additional, unexpected years.

In one of our early meetings about how to use her postdoctoral time, we discussed all of the different active projects of my research group, the Creative Computing Lab. Sarah, in her supportive and level style, listened as I rattled off idea after idea. And then she asked me, "What do you need to create?" I loved this question and all of the different directions it invited. I found myself dwelling on the idea of need. *Was this a professional need? A social need?*

I realized that it was a deeply personal need. I needed to write a book to share the possibilities of supporting self-direction for all learners, lifting up the beautiful and inspiring work already happening in public school classrooms and honoring the incredible pedagogical imaginations and efforts of K–12 teachers who are cultivating very different cultures of learning than are often available to young learners. Sarah, who thinks about and cares so deeply about teachers, students, and classrooms, was the ideal partner for this creation. I have learned so much from her over the past decade and through the process of developing this book together.

EXPLORING THE CLASSROOM AS DESIGN STUDIO

In this book, Sarah and I are inviting you into our exploration of the classroom as design studio, examining how teachers are supporting self-direction in their communities of K–12 learners. The remainder of part I explores the meaning and history of self-directed learning, explains how the need for better understanding of the relationship between support and self-direction led to our research study focused on teachers and classrooms, and describes the structure of the writing that resulted. Part II is the heart of the book: forty stories that illustrate the classroom as design studio. Each story is framed by a teacher's question, and begins with a vignette of classroom practice that demonstrates the classroom as design studio in action. We unpack each vignette with a theoretical text that helps us understand how that teacher is supporting self-direction in their classroom. In part III, Sarah and I look across these classroom portraits to share our understanding of how teachers support self-direction in the classroom as design studio, which we offer as one essential practice that teachers use to express and sustain six core commitments. Although we could have shared this framework at an earlier moment in the book—say, as part of this introduction or as a way to organize the forty stories—we felt it was important to first invite readers into a process of exploration and inquiry, creating space for you to experience the breadth of possibilities described in the stories and to engage in your own sensemaking about the classroom as design studio. Finally, after our shared writing, the book ends with an epilogue by Sarah in which she offers perspective as one teacher thinking through the meaning of these ideas for her own practice.

WHAT IS THE RELATIONSHIP BETWEEN SELF-DIRECTION AND SUPPORT?

Our offering of the classroom as design studio reflects our core belief in the interdependence between self-direction and support, when too often these concepts (and their importance to learning) have been seen as separate, or even contradictory. But what do we mean by *self-directed* learning? Why do we think it is so important? The most frequent contemporary uses of self-direction in education refer to it as a discrete skill, a desired outcome of learning experiences such as project- or problem-based learning, that will help young people succeed in college, the workforce, and life.[6] Yet we mean something more fundamental than a skill. We define a self-directed learner as someone who exercises individual agency and personal judgment in their activities—a self-directed learner makes decisions about what they learn and create, how they interact with others, and what their learning means to them. Self-direction is more than a skill; it is a way of being. We believe that self-direction enables learners to find joy and meaning in what they are doing, enhancing their learning in the moment and creating a virtuous cycle in which learners are excited to continue learning in the future.

(A BRIEF HISTORY OF) SELF-DIRECTION AND SUPPORT

In positioning our understanding of self-directed learning this way, we are more closely aligned with how the term was used in adult education in the 1960s and 1970s, most notably by American educator Malcolm Knowles in his 1975 book *Self-Directed Learning: A Guide for Learners and Teachers*. Knowles was motivated by the same reaction against factory models of education, by the same commitment to human thriving that was fueling the educational writing of countercultural figures such as John Holt and Carl Rogers.[7] He offered three key assertions about self-directed learning: self-directed learning can and does happen; the purpose of self-directed learning is to see one's self as capable of learning, both now and in the future; and the relationship between self-directed learning and more traditional teacher-directed learning represents a continuum rather than a dichotomy. These ideas are powerfully encapsulated in an early statement from Knowles to the reader:

> My motives are the motives of a missionary—so beware, I'll try to convert you. And therein lies also my main bias—at least the main bias that I am aware of: *I think that self-directed learning is the best way to learn.* I acknowledge that there are situations in which teaching, instruction, and even indoctrination are called for. But I also think that every act of teaching should have built into it some provision for helping the learner become more self-directing. I recognize that there are situations in which a person is indeed dependent in some respects, and that in these situations it is appropriate for them to be taught or directed. But I don't think that it is healthy—or even humane—for a person to be kept permanently dependent upon a system or another person.[8]

Much of the educational research on self-directed learning in the following decades focused on trying to name what did and did not count as self-directed learning, on quantifying self-directed learning, and on breaking it into its constituent parts in order to better measure if and when it was happening. However, the worry that such efforts were losing sight of what was valuable about self-directed learning prompted a critical reexamination of the term within adult education, including calls to focus on self-direction through more open-ended, creative, or exploratory tasks,[9] as well as on greater consideration of the broader impacts of self-direction, such as cultivating excitement for future learning and making meaning of one's life.[10]

That the foundational work on self-direction focused on adult education reflected historical beliefs that young people were less capable of, and less in need of, self-direction.[11] More recently, self-direction has been recognized as essential to learning across the lifespan. In particular, *How People Learn*, the National Research Council's widely acclaimed report published by the National Academies in 2000,[12] affirmed the importance of self-direction for young learners, arguing that children's desire for learning need not depend on external motivation, control, or reward, and that learners, even very young ones, have ideas about what they know, what they want to learn, and how they want to learn—ideas that should be acknowledged and supported in how their learning experiences are designed.

But what does it mean to support learners' own ideas? We believe that much of the difficulty in realizing the potential of self-directed learning over the last several decades has stemmed from the perceived contradiction between self-direction and support. There is a delicate and elusive balance between offering learners the freedom to pursue their own interests and providing enough support for learners to be successful. As reflected in foundational writing on student-centered learning, there has been ongoing confusion about whether learner agency and independence—with learners developing their own ideas about their work, about themselves, about how they best learn—benefit from, or are impeded by, teacher support and intervention. For example, progressive educators such as John Dewey and Paulo Freire have been misunderstood as minimizing the role of teachers, despite subsequent attempts to contradict and correct those misperceptions.[13]

Responding to this persistent misunderstanding, Malcolm Knowles argued that self-directed learning does not mean a lack of assistance or support—and in fact such support is necessary for becoming more self-directed. Similarly, although Canadian educator and researcher Allen Tough's seminal 1967 study about self-directed learning was titled *Learning Without a Teacher*, one of his central findings was that learners still needed and sought out many forms of assistance, including help knowing the kinds of resources to consult, the kinds of activities that might be valuable, and how to accurately assess progress, along with general emotional support for the fears and doubts that can accompany self-directed (or any) form of learning.[14] Learners are not always able to meaningfully choose for themselves the topics, forms, and paths of learning; the support of others can be essential in helping learners discover what holds meaning and value for them,[15] and in helping learners go beyond the limits of their own perspectives.[16]

But agreement on a learner-centered theory of learning has not meant agreement on a learner-centered theory of pedagogy.[17] Much of the ongoing debate about the efficacy and benefit of learner-centered pedagogical approaches has focused on the extent to which support is necessary and what that support might look like in the classroom.[18] The idea that teachers should provide support responsively has sometimes been caricatured as a total lack of support for their students.[19] And in turn, this caricature has sometimes been used to argue for direct instruction,[20] leaving little space for the expressions of agency and opportunities for personal meaning-making that characterize self-directed learning.

The complexity of the relationship between self-direction and support, and the lack of available models for what that support looks like,[21] led us to the research study that resulted in this book. Ultimately, supporting self-direction in the K–12 classroom involves intentional, thoughtful work on the part of the teacher, who navigates the nebulous space between total lack of support and total control over the learner. In this book, our goal is to shine a light on that beautiful and complex work, exploring how teachers create space for learners to have their own ideas and help them pursue those ideas in ways that feel connected and important to the learner, and supported by the classroom learning community. To do this, to understand the work of supporting self-direction, we needed to talk with teachers.

LEARNING FROM TEACHERS

This book was created through our experiences with twenty-five K–12 teachers who were supporting students' self-directed learning in their classrooms. As reflected in table I.1, the teachers we worked with represented different grade levels, regions within the United States, and teaching experience (although weighted toward more experienced teachers). While all of these teachers used computing in their classrooms in some

Table I.1 Demographic information of the participating teachers

Pseudonym	Grade band[a]	Geographic area	Teaching experience[b]	Title I support[c]
Alan	High	West	Late-career	No
Allison	Middle	Northeast	Mid-career	No
Ana	Middle	Midwest	Early-career	No
Andrea	Elementary	South	Mid-career	Yes
Benjamin	Elementary	South	Late-career	Yes
Betsy	Elementary	Midwest	Mid-career	No
Irene	High	Northeast	Late-career	No
Janet	Elementary	Midwest	Late-career	No
Jenny	Elementary	Midwest	Mid-career	No
Jess	Elementary	South	Mid-career	No
Jordan	Elementary	Northeast	Late-career	Yes
Kara	Elementary	Northeast	Mid-career	No
Karina	Elementary	West	Late-career	Yes
Katherine	High	Northeast	Late-career	No
Kelly	Elementary	South	Late-career	Yes
Kristine	Middle	West	Late-career	Yes
Leslie	Middle	Northeast	Late-career	No
Mary	Elementary	South	Late-career	Yes
Melanie	Elementary	Northeast	Late-career	Yes
Nathan	High	Northeast	Early-career	No
Penny	Middle	Midwest	Mid-career	No
Rose	High	Northeast	Late-career	Yes
Tamara	Middle	Northeast	Late-career	Yes
Tonya	Middle	South	Early-career	Yes
Torie	High	Northeast	Mid-career	No

[a] Typically, elementary indicates US grades K–5, middle indicates US grades 6–8, and high indicates US grades 9–12.

[b] We define an early-career teacher as having less than five years of teaching experience, mid-career as having five to ten years of teaching experience, and late-career as having more than ten years of teaching experience.

[c] Eleven teachers served students in schools with more than 40 percent of students from low-income families, which is a contributing consideration of Title I qualification.

way (reflecting a longstanding focus on computing education in our own research), there was a mix of general education teachers, STEAM lab and computer teachers, and other subject-area specialists. There was tremendous variety in their classroom practices and classroom contexts, from how beholden they were to curriculum and other content standards, to how much preparation they believed learners needed before being able to productively explore, to how much they intervened in projects as students were working.

We wanted to understand what teachers were doing but also what they felt was important, and how those values and their pedagogical practices were connected. Accordingly, we collected several different sources of data that gave us a window into teachers' thinking and work: teacher interviews, reflective journals, and classroom observations. Members of our research group, Laura Peters and Jane Kang, conducted an in-depth series of three interviews (collectively totaling approximately four hours of time) with each teacher, moving from their professional histories, through descriptions of their current pedagogical practices, and concluding with reflections on any ways in which their pedagogical aspirations and practices may have changed over the course of their participation in the research study, and what advice they had for other teachers who wanted to support similar approaches to learning in the classroom. The interviews drew from our observations of their classrooms, as well as artifacts teachers had collected and shared that illustrated aspects of their classroom practice, such as lesson plans, activity handouts, and samples of student work.

Two ideas came through clearly in the data, from the very beginning of our analysis. As we began the process of trying to make sense of this data, going through the interviews, journals, and observations to understand what was happening in these classrooms, we were struck by a recurring refrain: these teachers held a profound belief in learners' capacities to have their own ideas and to enact them in projects. That is, they believed that learners both could be and should be self-directed. And, seemingly counterintuitively, the teachers asserted that learners' incredible individual work depended critically on interactions with others—with teachers, with peers, and with the world beyond. They described different ways, through both formal and informal structures, that they created classroom cultures in which students were excited to share work and ideas and looked to one another as resources and inspiration. We noted that there was resonance here with our readings about self-directed learning. These teachers expressed both the importance of having your own ideas and the importance that others play in helping you realize those ideas. They were describing how support can enable self-direction to flourish. These ideas are the essence of what we want to call attention to by offering the metaphor of the classroom as design studio.

SHARING STORIES FROM CLASSROOMS

The heart of this book is a collection of forty stories of teachers supporting student self-direction in the classroom as design studio. Each has a similar structure: an opening question, a descriptive vignette of classroom practice, and a theoretically grounded analysis of the classroom activities presented. Table I.2 lists all of the questions, teachers and their grade bands, and theorists.

QUESTION

Each story is titled with a question. The questions are from teachers, primarily for their students, though a few times for themselves about their students. Most of the questions are direct language that we heard teachers use in their classrooms, or language that teachers reported or suggested during interviews or in their reflective journals. These are not questions that ask learners to recall information, or questions that pretend there is choice and autonomy when there is really only one answer. These are genuine questions: about learners, who they are, what they need, how they think, what they are trying to do. Teachers are asking about things that they don't know, but need to know in order to support students in their self-directed learning. The questions are addressed to students as people with ideas to be taken seriously—ideas about the work itself, ideas to share with others.

The importance of questioning in learning spaces has long been a preoccupation of ours: interest in what questions can open up and in what questions convey to learners about the power of their own ideas and thinking. In an early draft of the book, something clicked into place for

Table I.2 Overview of questions, teachers, and theorists

Questions	Teachers	Theorists
What are you interested in?	Kelly, elementary	Montessori
What's important to you?	Benjamin, elementary	Holt
What's your vision?	Nathan, high	Weick
What are some possible ideas?	Irene, high	Rinaldi
Do you think you know how to start?	Benjamin, elementary	Duckworth
What's a good thing that happened in your life this week?	Karina, elementary	Noddings
What's interesting about this?	Janet, elementary	Resnick
How could you use this for your own ideas?	Betsy, elementary	Ito
What do you want to do?	Jess, elementary	Giddens
Do you want to make any changes?	Jenny, elementary	Lave and Wenger
Would you like to stay and code with us this morning?	Kara, elementary	Bamberger, Duckworth, and Lampert
Can you help us learn?	Andrea, elementary	hooks
What can we make together?	Torie, high	Dewey
What do you want to build today?	Benjamin, elementary	Csikszentmihalyi
Why can't a bowl of noodles be a character?	Kara, elementary	Schön
What did you try?	Allison, middle	Vygotsky
Did you make the music come out like you wanted?	Tamara, middle	Lorde
That looks awesome! What will happen next?	Melanie, elementary	Freire
What's up?	Nathan, high	Froebel
What have others done?	Alan, high	Illich
Who doesn't get it at all?	Allison, middle	Dweck
What do you think?	Katherine, high	Rancière
What are you going to do now?	Rose, high	Hawkins

Table I.2 (continued)

Questions	Teachers	Theorists
What can you make with it?	Ana, middle	Franklin
How can we fix it?	Penny, middle	Papert
Does anyone want to share?	Jordan, elementary	Dewey
Who discovered the coolest things?	Kelly, elementary	Turkle and Papert
What are other people doing?	Jordan, elementary	McDermott and Varenne
Did you ask your neighbor?	Tonya, middle	Rogoff
Would you like to do that?	Jess, elementary	Ryan and Deci
Can you teach that to me?	Mary, elementary	Postman and Weingartner
You've got this, right?	Leslie, middle	Ladson-Billings
What are you trying to do?	Melanie, elementary	Rogers
What do you expect of yourself?	Irene, high	Giroux
What does this mean to you?	Rose, high	Hall
What does quality mean to you?	Penny, middle	Calkins
What would you like to showcase?	Kristine, middle	Shulman
What were your struggles?	Janet, elementary	Turkle
What would you have done if you had more time?	Ana, middle	Piaget
What do you see?	Jordan, elementary	Rinaldi

us when we tried titling each story with a question. It was both the practice of questioning itself and the specifics of what teachers were asking learners that finally crystallized a core idea we had been circling around: in the classroom as design studio, teachers do an incredible amount of work to center students, helping learners figure out what they want to do and how they want to do it.

Amid everything we offer here about teaching and learning, the most essential is this: start with questions.

VIGNETTE

Following each question is a vignette from one teacher's classroom. These brief accounts illustrate teaching and learning in the classroom as design studio—what it looks like and feels like, what teachers and learners are doing, and how they are interacting with one another. Some vignettes focus on a particular moment, while others offer glimpses over time. They represent specifics of student and teacher language and of particular prompts and projects.

Despite all of the detail and specificity we offer about these twenty-five classrooms across these forty vignettes, we have purposefully removed all references to specific technological tools, specific programming languages, and specific software platforms. We did this, in part, because technologies come and go and can make writing quickly feel dated. But more importantly, we removed these references because this is not a book about technology or even about computing education: it is a book about learning. Accordingly, we focus on what is powerful in the learning experience. The tools and subject matter may enable aspects of this learning, but the learning is not wholly dependent upon them.

It is often hard for people to believe (even when they want to) that this kind of open-ended, self-directed work is possible—especially within public K–12 education, or especially with young learners, or especially within high school classrooms, or especially with fixed disciplinary commitments and requirements. The teachers and classrooms of this study were very different from each other, not just in student age, subject matter, and geographic setting, but also in personal style and pedagogical approach. While there was a shared commitment across the teachers to some concept of open-ended projects and to taking learners and their ideas seriously, the teachers differed in the amount of openness and unstructured exploration they designed in learning experiences for their students.

Although these vignettes aren't intended as a prescription or a how-to guide, we believe that they demonstrate pedagogical possibilities within a wide variety of settings. This variety among teachers and classrooms is reflective of our belief and argument that supporting self-direction doesn't only look or work one way. We hope that many different types of teachers can find themselves in this collection, resonating with particular aspirations and classroom practices that they can imagine themselves engaging in. In the classroom as design studio, just as learners must have the space to be themselves and to make the work their own, we as teachers must be able to be ourselves and to make the work our own.

We share these stories of classrooms and teachers not only to show what's possible, but also because we find them inspirational—and hope that others will as well. We love the specificity and diversity of what students make, how they talk about what the work means to them, and the questions they ask their classmates about their work. We are inspired by the work of the teachers, by the projects they design that advance learners' conceptual understandings and support rigorous exploration of content while simultaneously inviting learners to have their own ideas and express who they are. We appreciate how the teachers enable learners to enter into this open-ended work, thoughtfully intervening when students are struggling and enabling them to move forward but not telling them what to do. We admire the distinct culture of learning these teachers create in their classrooms, the sense of collective investment in each other's work, the feeling that all members of the classroom community are simultaneously teachers and learners, trying to understand things themselves and supporting others in doing so. We are inspired by the language teachers use with students, by the questions that prompt learners back to the work and to their own ideas, responding in moments of difficulty by reminding learners of their enormous wealth of internal resources.

THEORY

We initially drafted these vignettes using just the collected data: the teacher interviews, reflective journals, and classroom observations. For each classroom, we had some sense of the ideas we wanted to share and why those ideas were especially significant or powerful. But we felt that we needed additional support to fully articulate the power of the ideas we were seeing in the vignettes. To that end, we decided to pair each classroom vignette with a theoretical text. Many of these texts, though not all of them, were written by people within the field of education broadly—teachers, researchers, philosophers—especially those who might be identified as belonging to *progressive* or *critical* traditions. While the writings of progressive educators and critical theorists have been central to each of our intellectual and professional trajectories, we do not expect that the same is necessarily true of our readers. But we hope that all readers might find inspiration and utility in these theories.

These texts and authors have been meaningful to us in thinking about what is most important in teaching and learning, in helping us formulate the metaphor of the classroom as design studio. We find their words beautiful, capturing concepts and feelings that can be difficult to express. While these authors were writing in many different contexts, we felt that each had something important to say about supporting self-direction. These authors have contributed to our understanding of what it looks like and feels like for learners to be in classrooms where the focus is on their own ideas, where they make decisions about what is best for their own learning process, where they figure out how to do things they haven't done before, and where they learn with and from others. These authors have also contributed to our understanding of how teachers support those processes.

The theoretical works we draw upon span more than two hundred years. That each of the authors we include was writing from a specific cultural and historical moment is sometimes reflected in a narrowness of who they thought they were writing for and about. For example, some of the texts include unnecessarily gendered language, reflecting an assumption of the male (and presumably white and Western) identity as the universal one. We debated whether to update pronouns in quoted material. We ultimately decided to leave the source material almost entirely unchanged, but we wanted to acknowledge our commitment to inclusion here. The theorists we have selected are not the only voices who could have been brought in to speak about supporting self-direction, about creation within community, about taking learners and their ideas seriously. But they are voices that have been central to our own work as researchers and practitioners, helping us to understand and make sense of what we are doing and what we are trying to do. While there are many others we wished to include, we sometimes struggled with a lack of resonance between texts we loved and the classroom vignettes we loved. We are curious about what connections others will see, about alternative theories and theorists that could illuminate the classroom work portrayed here.

Educational research has struggled to bring together practice and theory, to have these two worlds inform and enrich each other. We worry when we see research that talks at teachers, not with them. With this book, and the research study that informed it, we have aspired to learn from teachers in order to give back to teachers. There are wonderful things happening in classrooms. But, as the teachers we spoke with expressed, they too often happen in isolation—isolation that keeps teachers from sharing what they know and from learning more about what they don't yet know, to the detriment of individual teachers and the field as a whole. Teachers want to connect to others who care about similar things, and learn from others' practices.

Theory can help us combat this isolation. It can make us feel less alone in what we care about and in our struggles to turn those commitments into the design of classrooms and learning experiences. It gives us shared language for understanding and discussing what classroom teachers are aspiring to and actually doing. It is, as poet and literary theorist Kenneth Burke said of literature, "equipment for living."[22] We bring in these theorists to help name not only what teachers are doing, but why it is important, to help us understand what is meaningful and valuable in their classrooms. Theory can be used as a way of appreciating, rather than tearing down. Theoretical lenses also help us broaden our perspectives. The classroom stories, by design, have a specific, narrow focus. When we fold in theory, we are better equipped to see alternatives, to imagine the consequences of other ways of doing things, to envision what is at stake in enacting the classroom as design studio.

As such, theory can be of tremendous value in helping us manage the multiple practical demands and pressures of daily life in the classroom by encouraging clarity about our goals and values. Having a goal such as "I want to take learners and their ideas seriously" or "I want to support learners in being self-directed" or "I want my students to believe in themselves as people capable of creation" doesn't tell us exactly what to do in a given situation or exactly what practices to invoke. But that clarity can help us formulate ideas about what to do, make decisions between possibilities, and adjust course when things don't go as planned.

Of course, as teachers, we do also need concrete ideas and images of the kinds of practices that are possible. We paired classroom stories and theoretical texts so that they can inform and enrich each other. Our intention is that, in concert, the vignette and the theory jointly clarify an idea about self-directed learning in the classroom. We make these connections between practice and theory in different ways across the collection. Sometimes the resonance or connection is very clear and straightforward, and that clarity is itself what we are offering: here is a tangible example of what theory says is important and what it looks like. Or here is how teachers themselves are talking about what they are doing and why, and here is a theoretical framework that reinforces the value of those beliefs and actions. But sometimes the relationship between the classroom and the theory is more metaphorical than concrete. Here we are putting a particular theory in conversation with a particular classroom because it pulls our attention somewhere important, somewhere that might not have been clear from the classroom story alone.

We want the structure of the book itself—organized as a collection of stories composed of questions, vignettes, and theories—to signal that the classroom as design studio can be realized in many different ways. Rather than organizing around a select set of strategies or concepts, we present our book as a mosaic. The depth of the work does not reside in any single story; the depth, we hope, is a product of the breadth—a picture that unfolds across a curated collection of many teachers, many theorists. The recurrence of ideas across the stories creates a kind of cumulative complementarity that we think is incredibly important. The ideas manifest in multiple ways and the different classrooms demonstrate multiple perspectives on these ideas. We also believe that providing a diverse array of concise, interconnected stories defends against the potential for any one story to feel prescriptive, a "right way" to do this work. We hope many different types of teachers will be able to see themselves reflected in this work, either in what they are currently doing or in what they might be inspired to try in their practice, even in very small or incremental ways.

We have sequenced this collection of stories purposefully, following a general learning process that we saw teachers and their students engaging in. Though to call this a "process" is in no way to suggest a linear process; teachers and students were engaging in these different kinds of thinking, doing, and being continuously and iteratively, moving back and forth from one part of the learning process to another. We begin with questions that invite learners into the work, encouraging students to define their goals and vision and highlighting the importance of making the work their own. The next, longest stretch is what we call the "messy middle": questions that reflect teachers and learners navigating the complexity of trying to make their visions real, figuring out how to do things, determining the kinds of supports they might need to do so, interacting with others around their own work, sharing ideas and inspiration, and working through the inevitable challenges that arise. And, finally, we end with questions that invite learners to take a step back and consider what the work they have done means to them, what they think of it, and what they might do differently in the future.

Perhaps unsurprisingly, we encourage you to engage with this collection in whatever way feels meaningful to you. You may want to read the collection from start to finish. Or you may want to just jump in somewhere, with a question that provokes your curiosity, a classroom context that seems similar to your own, or a theorist who is calling to you. We invite you to begin, following the guidance of one of our teachers: *Like you want. Any way you want.*

II

QUESTIONS

WHAT ARE YOU INTERESTED IN?

"What are you interested in? What do you care about?" elementary STEAM teacher Kelly asks the first graders who have gathered on the rug in her classroom. These questions are the entry point into a sustained, six-week passion project, in which these young learners will define and pursue a research topic of their choosing, culminating in the creation of a physical product. While every aspect of the project is chosen by the learners themselves, Kelly designs supports and structures that enable these six- and seven-year-olds to meaningfully engage with their topics and make their ideas real.

Kelly begins by scheduling initial planning conferences with each student. In these meetings, Kelly and the student talk about what the student wants to research. Based on these conversations, Kelly prepares a collection of resources to support students as they start their investigations. She presents each student with a notebook where they can use their emerging literacy to keep track of their work: a place for notes and lists of ideas, books, videos, and people. As students get further into their research, they generate more refined questions and find resources to help them answer those questions. Kelly uses the notebooks to support her weekly progress check-ins with each student, getting a sense of where they are in their process and talking to them about what they need to move forward.

Students' interests and pathways to exploring their interests vary widely. One learner, motivated by the importance of a recent local Rodeo Day, focuses on horses. She interviews a large animal veterinarian and curates websites that relate to horses and horse breeding. For her project, she draws a gallery full of portraits of different kinds of horses. Another student is investigating the migration behaviors of monarch butterflies between Canada and Mexico. She paints a giant map, makes physical butterflies out of recycled materials, and places the butterflies at significant points on the map to show their migration patterns. A third student focuses on her own family, interviewing relatives to develop a family history. In her notebook, she draws a full body picture of each person and keeps all of her interview notes related to that person.

As the research projects build toward a culminating event in which the first graders will display their projects to one another, Kelly asks them to imagine how they could show their classmates what they have learned while they are simultaneously moving around the room to look at other people's projects. The class converges on the idea of using a programming environment they have recently explored to create animated versions of their projects that could be displayed without their presence. The first graders use this environment to create these digital versions of their physical projects—experimenting with the image library and drawing tools, recording narrations, and learning to cope with the heartbreak of accidental deletions.

While students set up their gallery of passion projects in physical and digital formats, Kelly records videos of her students talking about their work and what it means to them. A student beams as she describes her work: "This is my personal project just about my family. I asked them about their childhood and their adulthood. I asked them what I should know about them. And I wrote, by myself, what I loved about them. Then I made a project that shows all the facts from my interviews. It made me so happy!"

Throughout this book, we, as authors, offer connections between teachers' classroom work and theoretical texts that can illuminate that work and its significance. But in our conversations with Kelly, she made the connection between her work and the writings of Italian early childhood educator and theorist Maria Montessori, framing the value of this first-grade passion project in terms of the ideas about learning she saw in Montessori's work.

> The perfect Montessori is the prepared environment. And that is the absolute dream for this room. The prepared environment where they are pursuing their own interests and passions, and I am introducing tools and skills. I mean, it's very time intensive. I'm so proud of me for stepping back and just preparing the environment. And I think Maria would be proud of me![1]

In this quote we see Kelly meaningfully and productively making sense of theory for her daily practice: a century-old text and its author are dynamic, living tools for imagining, planning, enacting, and reflecting on the design of learning experiences for her students.

Specifically, Kelly referenced Montessori's idea of the *prepared environment,* the classroom as a thoughtfully and carefully designed space in which the available materials and structures support learners in their independent explorations. In our discussions, she further emphasized three important, and interrelated, classroom practices for supporting her first graders' projects, all of which she saw as resonant with Montessori's theory and approach—and all of which are consistent with our framing of the classroom as design studio in this book. Most importantly, this is a project driven by learners' interests, by the things they care about. As Montessori described in her writing, what we are drawn to in the world around us is both an expression of ourselves and an aid to our enactment of ourselves. By giving them the space to, as Kelly says, pursue their own interests and passions, she enables learners to make consequential decisions about how they learn and what they create. This is built into the structure of the independent research project, in which the first graders take a broad interest (such as butterflies or family) and turn it into specific questions, things they want to understand, actions they can take to further that understanding, and choices about how to express that understanding in physical and digital design. Montessori highlighted the importance of decisions to the development of the self, to the need for independence that she saw as critical to learning. In her 1917 text *Spontaneous Activity in Education,* she wrote that "our entire life is a continual exercise of decisions. . . . The stronger we are in such exercises, the more independent we shall be of others. Clarity of ideas, the mechanism of the habit of decision, give us a sense of liberty."[2]

Kelly noted the connection between this independence and her decision to "step back" in her role as teacher, a change that she ascribed to Montessori's influence on her teaching practice. Montessori emphasized the need for the teacher to not impose themselves on the spontaneous activity of the child, to observe rather than immediately intervene, to only offer words, ideas, and objects to help learners move forward along the paths they set for themselves. Kelly explained that this was both a central goal for her teaching and also something that she struggled with. In describing what she most wanted of herself in the coming year, she shared a desire for:

> Just more front-loading, more preparing the environment, more taking that time to trust them to do enough on their own. And it's so hard to know what

> the difference is between helping and taking over, because that line is different for every, every child. They're working on something, and I'm like, "Oh, I have an idea." So that is my personal goal next year, to really be making sure that I am looking out for that line, more and more.

The tension Kelly surfaced here, between helping and taking over, is familiar to all of us as teachers. In her design and execution of this project, we see Kelly striking a careful balance that respects Montessori's guidance regarding teacher intervention. The learners' own ideas are at the center and her students are making meaningful and consequential decisions about what they are doing and how they are doing it. This is their project, not hers. But Kelly's support and structure are substantive and necessary. She conferences with students, talking to them about what they are interested in, what they want to understand, and how they can do it. She directs them to initial resources that help them get started. She provides them with notebooks that increase their sense of ownership and enable productive note-taking. Kelly's presence enables rather than impedes learners' expressions of self and development of future independence.

Kelly offered that one of the reasons she can step back in this way is the internal motivation that fuels these projects: her students want to learn and work because they are interested in and excited about what they are doing. She spoke about how this project grew out of her own desire to find something where "*they* want to continue to work. Something where *I'm* not the one going, 'Well, what else does it do? And is that it? And that's all you can do?'" Kelly noted that this motivation was evidenced by the steady focus the first graders showed throughout the project, flagging neither in attention nor determination over a long period, not needing something new to engage them, fulfilled by going deeper into the topics they cared about. The use of sustained, uninterrupted time in the learning environment, reflecting patience on the part of both learner and teacher, is one of the defining characteristics of a Montessori classroom. Montessori analogized the callousness with which we often interrupt young people in their work to someone shouting at a mathematician, a painter, or a poet to stop what they are doing in the middle of their process of creation. When we push learners onto the next class, the next project, the next activity, we are interrupting them in the process of becoming themselves.

At the heart of these practices—foregrounding learners' interests, stepping back as teachers, giving time—is a conviction that even the youngest of learners are people with ideas to be taken seriously. As Montessori wrote in her 1912 text *The Montessori Method*:

> We cannot know the consequences of suffocating a *spontaneous action* at the time when the child is just beginning to be active: perhaps we suffocate *life itself*. Humanity shows itself in all its intellectual splendor during this tender age as the sun shows itself at the dawn, and the flower in the first unfolding of the petals; and we must *respect* religiously, reverently, these first indications of individuality. If any educational act is to be efficacious, it will be only that which tends to *help* toward the complete unfolding of this life.[3]

This belief stood in contrast to contemporary views that characterized young people as incomplete, with the purpose of school to fill in what they did not know and could not do. While many of Montessori's practices have been widely adopted, those practices have sometimes been implemented without attention to this underlying belief. All of the elements of Kelly's classroom that she noted as important, elements that help learners develop their ideas and develop faith in themselves as people with ideas, are grounded in this conviction. As Kelly explained, "The minute I push in with my, 'Well, how about this way?' I devalue what they're doing." Montessori's writing is full of passionate arguments against a deficit model of childhood, against dismissing or denying what very young people are capable of. She cautions against what is lost when we do not offer learners space and support to explore and express the unique, complex, and powerful selves within them. Montessori's ideas and their instantiation within Kelly's classroom invite us as teachers to think expansively about the freedom and responsibility young learners are capable of managing—and then to create opportunities for our students to do more, to be more, than we can even imagine.

WHAT'S IMPORTANT TO YOU?

Elementary STEM lab teacher Benjamin is excited to have his second graders start working with a more advanced version of a visual programming language that they had first used as kindergarteners. He is interested in the expanded avenues for expression the students will be able to find in the broadened set of features. But he recognizes that with greater possibilities comes the chance of feeling overwhelmed, and so he plans an introductory project in which they can begin their explorations. In this activity, he invites his students to create projects about themselves. He introduces this project through a quick demonstration of the animation he has created about himself, showing how to add visual elements (drawing some, choosing some from the library) and how to make those elements interactive.

After sharing his project, Benjamin invites his second graders to think about their projects, asking them, "What's important to you? What do you want to share about yourself?" The students have many ideas about things they are interested in, eagerly naming elements they might want to include in their programs. Students excitedly begin to shout out things that they like, and then move into more specific details about things that are important to them that they want to represent in a project that is all about them. "I have three brothers and sisters!" "I really love to do this with my family!" "This is my favorite place to go!"

But as students transition into creating their own projects, some hesitation creeps in. Somewhat cautiously, they ask Benjamin to confirm that they can make whatever they want, that the purpose of the project is actually to express the things they have thought of in a way that works for them. "We can make anything? Like, anything, anything?" Benjamin responds, "I really mean anything.

You can use this tool to express whatever ideas, whatever thoughts, whatever anything you want to share. It is entirely up to you. Really, it's up to you!"

Being able to make choices for yourself, choices about what projects you create and how you create those projects, is an essential aspect of the classroom as design studio. Benjamin explained to us why this was a core element of his classroom, framing it in terms of what he wanted learners to understand about themselves:

> It says that creativity and individual choice, ideas, voice, are valued in this classroom. Not just when we're doing a particular project, not just when it's time to do an expo or a showcase project once a year or whatever, not just at particular times, but every day in this classroom. You are going to have the opportunity to make a choice about how things look, how they work, what you're going to look at, do, the tools you're going to use. You don't get all the choices, but every day you're going to have a chance to choose what you're doing and make things look the way you want. Every day you're going to have a voice, and that voice is valued in this room.

When Benjamin asks his students, "What's important to you?," when he invites them to create projects in which they choose what they want to share about themselves and how they want to represent it, he is telling them that their ideas and judgment matter, that they have weight in the learning environment. This is what it means to make choices. Yet, as we see here, while that freedom to choose can be valued and welcomed by students, it can also be met with uncertainty and skepticism, with worry. As part of the structured group discussion at the beginning of class, students are excited to share their ideas, naming the elements of their lives they want to include in their projects. When they break off to work on turning their ideas into tangible projects, the second graders are unsure that this opportunity is genuine, wondering whether there's actually a "right" answer lurking somewhere that they are supposed to produce, rather than following their interests.

In a trilogy of passionate, provocative books written between 1964 and 1972 (*How Children Fail*, *How Children Learn*, and *Freedom and Beyond*), American educator John Holt attacked what he described as the destructive dominance of being right and wrong in school. His conviction was that when learning is framed as the pursuit of an answer someone else has determined, this produces so much anxiety (about being right) and fear (of being wrong) that no actual learning can occur. Holt argued that what enables students to get out of this unproductive bind is pursuing their own interests. In learning situations where young people are invited to be genuinely curious, exploring something for their own ends, the anxiety of producing the right answer doesn't dominate and meaningful learning can take place. But just as we see with Benjamin's students, Holt noted that while offering choice as a way to enable students to pursue their own interests is powerful, it is also complex.

Holt argued that reactions like the skepticism and uncertainty expressed by Benjamin's students result from a two-fold lack of trust. First, students may not trust the invitation to choose. As Holt wrote, after we have offered "students some freedom, choice, and control in their learning, they [can] show us that they do not believe or trust us."[4] From Holt's era of the 1960s and 1970s to the present day, many students experience K–12 classrooms as highly structured and teacher-directed environments; students' interests and choices are too often not prioritized. And so, for students who are newly invited into making choices about their learning, there is understandable uncertainty. Second, students may lack trust in themselves. Even in classrooms where student choice is common practice, making those choices can nonetheless feel intimidating. As Holt asserted, "To choose is to risk."[5] When someone else is making choices for you, it may feel less exciting, but also less risky. If you fail at a task, you can reframe that failure as attributable to someone else's choices, rather than to your own. Students who haven't had opportunities to practice making choices for themselves may understandably lack the necessary self-confidence and self-trust to take a leap into the intellectual unknown, to pursue their interests, questions, and curiosities.

Benjamin sees this reaction in his students, and is conscious of working intentionally to respond to it. Noting that he is able to see changes across time because he works with students over multiple years, across grade levels, he explained to us:

When I started, everybody wanted to have the right way. I would say, "We're gonna learn these skills, and then you're gonna make something with it." And then it's, "Like this? Like this? Is this right? What do I do next? Is it this?" And "Is this what I'm supposed to be doing?" So it's an ongoing struggle to keep them willing to take chances on something that might not work.

In this vignette, we see Benjamin addressing this struggle in different ways. First, he is intentional in how choice is introduced. In his introductory activity, Benjamin's students all work with the same programming environment and on the same type of project. By constraining the tool selection and activity genre in this way, he avoids overloading students with too much choice, creating a safe foundation upon which students can explore their individual interests. Next, Benjamin perseveres in his commitment to student choice, despite their initial reactions. As Holt said, we must "keep our offer of freedom and choice on the table even though at first it is not believed or trusted."[6] Benjamin offers necessary reassurance that his invitation to choice is sincere, responding to his students' expressions of uncertainty by telling them "Really, it's up to you." This small act of reassurance is essential; it explicitly and implicitly communicates to students the legitimacy of their concerns about undertaking the work, and his confidence in their ability to be successful.

Benjamin described how, as his second-grade students began embracing the idea that they could really make whatever they wanted, following their interests led them to discoveries about the programming environment itself. For instance, some students remarked to Benjamin that they couldn't find a specific image in the built-in image library. Benjamin responded by suggesting that they could try to draw the character or object that they were imagining. With this prompt, students began experimenting with drawing tools, creating images that reflected their own visions and, in the process, learning how to do something that they hadn't done before. This is what choice in the classroom makes possible: it creates opportunities for learning that are motivated by what we care about, what we are interested in. In *How Children Fail*, Holt's first book arguing fervently that education should be driven by children's sense of what is important to them, he spoke to the power of this learning:

> It is not subject matter that makes some learning more valuable than others, but the spirit in which the work is done. . . . A child who is learning naturally, following his curiosity where it leads him, adding to his mental model of reality whatever he needs and can find a place for, and rejecting without fear or guilt what he does not need, is growing—in knowledge, in the love of learning, and in the ability to learn.[7]

WHAT'S YOUR VISION?

Most of the students in Nathan's high school web design class are new to coding and computer science. In structuring a project in which his students will design and then code their own website, Nathan thinks about how to support them in bridging the gap between what they want to do and what they are currently able to do. He begins with a simple prompt: "What's your vision?" This starting place, which is an entirely separate part of the assignment from the coding, encourages students to think through their ideas and plan out what they want to do. Nathan asks them to write about an imagined client for whom they are producing the website and an imagined audience who will use it. He reminds them to think through the stylistic choices they are going to make in light of those decisions—the colors, fonts, layout, and style of language. Finally, each student creates a simple prototype of their website, an image reflecting their vision for the design.

Once they have the prototype, Nathan encourages them to have fun with it. He advises them, "Be easy on yourselves. If you can't figure it out, it's okay to change your mind and do something that you can do." Students respond to this framing enthusiastically, jumping into the process of figuring out how to enact their visions in code. One student, inspired by a love of World War II history, creates a website dedicated to Rosie the Riveter. She is excited to share information about a topic she cares about and is also intrigued by the opportunity to try something new with color, incorporating bright primary colors and nontraditional typefaces into her design. Another student is especially proud of the unusual transition effect she creates when users click from one page to another. A third student finds that the design she laid out in her mock-up necessitates a navigation bar at the top of the page. She spends a long period of time, assisted by Nathan, figuring out how to code the idea she has in her mind.

Nathan was intentional in his use of the planning phase in this project, including his requirement that students prototype their websites before starting to code. He explained to us:

> It allows the students to think about "What do I want to create?" without at the same time having to think about how they will code it or even if they can code it. Then, when they start coding, it is just about "How do I make it happen?"

Here Nathan gestures to two important insights about what it is like for learners to engage in the process of defining and realizing their ideas in the classroom as design studio. The first is that planning gives an idea weight. Because they have spent the time carefully thinking about the websites they want to create, including details of who the sites are for and what they will look like, students are invested in their projects. He noted that this was especially important for learners who were new to coding and felt uncertain about the work, explaining that once they begin to have an actual vision "they start thinking more about what they're creating and less about what they're coding." Second, as we see in this vignette, this investment in planning motivates learners to take on greater challenges in the technical realm than they may have imagined they could. Nathan is conscious of the complex relationship between having ideas and making those ideas concrete, that the process of doing so involves a continual push and pull between aspiration and the realities of enactment. The permission Nathan gives his students to adjust as they go, his encouragement to have fun with their vision rather than have it operate as a punishingly unattainable goal, creates a space in which students may actually be able to exceed their own expectations for what they are able to do. Nathan describes the experience as a "confidence builder," explaining that he most values students learning "that they can do coding. That it's possible that they can get good at it, because most of them don't have any expectation that they're going to be good at it."

Nathan doesn't want his students to get bogged down or discouraged by technical difficulties and lose sight of what it is that they are trying to do. He also doesn't want them to treat their plan and prototype as sacred. Instead, he wants them to be open to what feels possible and doable in the moment, and to make adjustments as might be needed, while still guided by their vision. He wants them to engage in what American psychologist and organizational theorist Karl Weick described as the dynamic process of *sensemaking*: constantly attempting to state what things mean to us but also continually open to how information and inputs might change that meaning. In his 1995 book *Sensemaking in Organizations*, Weick related a favorite story to highlight what he argued was a fundamental component of sensemaking. In this story, a Hungarian army reconnaissance unit becomes lost in a snowstorm in the Alps. After three days, they return to their lieutenant and compatriots and explain that they were able to find their way back using a map that one of them discovered he had in his pocket. When their lieutenant examines the map, he sees that it is of an entirely different mountain range than the one in which the unit had been lost. Weick noted that "this incident raises the intriguing possibility that when you are lost, any old map will do,"[8] and he goes on to explain:

> The soldiers were able to produce a good outcome from a bad map because they were active, they had a purpose (get back to camp), and they had an image of where they were and where they were going. They kept moving, they kept noticing cues, and they kept updating their sense of where they were. As a result, an imperfect map proved to be good enough.[9]

While this example is deliberately provocative, the metaphor of an "imperfect map" that nevertheless enables someone to find their way helps us understand what Nathan is inviting his students to understand about the role of planning and prototyping in their creative processes. The prototype reflects their purpose, an image of what they are trying to do. It invites them to engage in a process of figuring things out. But it isn't something they should feel beholden to, or follow unreflectively. As they work to realize their visions, Nathan wants his students to be continually attentive to the cues Weick mentioned, to the information they are getting about what is and isn't working and why, which might suggest to them a need to adjust course or an affirmation to continue forward with determination.

This dynamic process of sensemaking is crucial because neither Nathan nor his students know at the outset exactly what creations will result from their design processes, or exactly what questions, stumbling blocks, and unexpected directions might emerge from their work. He tries to help them navigate this uncertainty by encouraging them to articulate purposes and plans that can guide them but not constrain them. Karl Weick's body of work is an exploration of what enables people and organizations to productively engage with the kinds of situations of uncertainty and ambiguity that characterize the classroom as design studio. He wrote about the tendency to want to close off this uncertainty, conscious of the allure of a predictable system of inputs and outputs, clearly delineated behaviors, and knowable decision points, which he termed "tightly coupled systems." One example that he offered of a tightly coupled system is a nuclear power plant; the predictability of the system and its components are what makes it possible to minimize the potential for catastrophe. Yet, in speaking specifically of schools, he wrote, "Seldom do people step aside long enough to realize that the task of educating is simply not the kind of task that can be performed in a tightly coupled system."[10] In contrast, he argued for the need of "loosely coupled systems" for supporting work such as teaching and learning, systems that are "more elusive, less tangible, harder to grasp, and harder to administer. The loose structure preserves novel solutions, facilitates local accommodations, and meets professional needs for autonomy."[11]

Weick argued that the distinct work of learning necessitates this kind of organization, but also that these very same qualities are often thrown back at schools and classrooms as failings. He posited that what enables loosely coupled organizations to be successful is the combination of clarity about vision—about what values, goals, and ideas are most important in the work being done—and continual responsiveness to the environment, enacted through thoughtful attention to what is actually going on and a willingness to dynamically adjust when things don't go as planned. In the loosely coupled system of a classroom, people act independently and autonomously, and the work of a teacher like Nathan is not to control behavior or ensure one way of doing things, but rather to help learners understand the meaning of what they are doing and make thoughtful decisions about how to pursue their goals. As a result, those learners have the chance to develop their own sense of what is important to them and what they might want to learn.

WHAT ARE SOME POSSIBLE IDEAS?

The Advanced Placement (AP) Computer Science Principles (CSP) course culminates with the Create Task, a component of the AP exam in which students demonstrate integrated understanding of the course material by developing a coding project of their choosing. Irene is excited for her AP CSP students to have the opportunity to develop this larger, self-directed project. But she knows that this project is much more open-ended than any other projects the class has done—and she wonders how she can best support them in this novel type of work.

Although she knows her students are full of ideas, she appreciates that articulating and developing meaningful ideas is complex and may potentially feel difficult to her students. In response, she designs a process for idea generation that involves several different activities and takes place over multiple weeks, enabling students to explore and consider different options before focusing on their choice.

At the start of the term, she explains the trajectory of the course, previewing the work that will be involved in the Create Task. Then, a few weeks before the Create Task launch, Irene introduces the practice of open-ended idea generation. As the students come into the classroom, they see a projected slide that says, "What are some possible ideas you have for your upcoming project?" Her students take a few minutes to write down some ideas and share with a neighbor. Closer to the project launch, Irene again introduces another prompt for ideating, inviting her students to think about projects they could make that would help improve their day. The students generate many ideas, playfully building on each other's suggestions, with the class-wide list serving as a demonstration of the wide range of project possibilities.

Through this process, Irene's students start to focus on ideas for projects that they really want to do. Two students start to design an if/then adventure game, using their own school as a setting. Two other students plan out an application about warning signs for domestic violence, presenting different scenarios that users can respond to. Finally, at the start of the Create Task, Irene shares a curated collection of previous students' projects, encouraging her students to critically consider these examples and how they might inform their own ideas and projects.

Time is essential to the work of the classroom as design studio; it is a resource that is vital to manifesting creative ideas. Students need time to make things they care about, certainly, but they also crucially need time to figure out what those things might be in the first place. Irene focuses our attention on the importance of time for her students' idea generation, and our view into her classroom highlights several strategies for supporting this necessary incubation time. First, she starts early. At the beginning of the term, she signals to students the nature of the work ahead of them, recognizing the unfamiliarity of this type of open-ended, self-directed task. And several weeks before her students are to begin the Create Task, Irene helps students plant seeds for potential project ideas. She designs small ways for them to engage with emergent ideas, even when the focus of the class is on something else, even if all they can do is say, "I have no idea what I'll create." Second, she structures a series of different tasks to help students engage in their idea generation, to give them different possible entry points. Rather than relying solely on totally unstructured time, she employs a range of strategies to help students surface project ideas that are rooted in their experiences and interests, from open-ended brainstorming, to responding to structured prompts, to examining curated examples. Finally, Irene allocates time both for individual work and for collective work in support of idea generation. She creates opportunities for students to dwell in their own and others' thinking and ideas.

Reggio Emilia (developed in Reggio Emilia, Italy, following World War II) is an approach to early childhood education that centers the agency and curiosity of young learners, and honors the multiplicity of their approaches to learning and being, their "100 languages" of expression.[12] In a series of interviews first published in 2006, Carlina Rinaldi, the longtime Reggio

Emilia educator and president of Reggio Children, Loris Malaguzzi International Centre, invited a critical examination and reimagining of time in learning. She questioned whether how we understand and use time in schools and classrooms is perhaps fundamentally misaligned with what it means to learn and how we think about the purpose of schools.

Today there is too little talk about schools and time. For me it is important that for a school to be a place of life, then it needs the time of life, and that time of life is different, for example, to the time of production. In production, the most important element is the product. But, as we said already, in a school what is important is the process, the path we develop. The educational relation needs to be able to make time, it needs to be slow, it needs empty time. . . . Is it legitimate today, when everything seems to go towards ever greater speed, in fact towards super-speed, to admire slowness, empty time, pauses? It is not a contest between speed and slowness, but about having the courage to rediscover the time of human beings.[13]

In Irene's classroom, we see a deep honoring of process, dedicating time to support the complexity of creation. Irene's choices embody the courage that Rinaldi described, creating space for her students to experience the process of engaging in creative acts.

One of the core ideas of the Reggio Emilia approach and, in turn, of Rinaldi's work is that children must be thought of as whole people and that learning must be considered in terms of the needs of human beings. In our conversations with her, Irene spoke about her different ways of using time not as something needed by students in the particular setting of school, but as something that all human beings need to engage in creative work. She knew, from her own experiences in the role of learner-creator, how much she benefited from time to think and reflect—and how frustrated she felt in its absence.

I don't like to pressure kids, just as I don't like to be pressured to come up with an idea. I hate it if I'm in a day-long workshop and they're like, "Now you guys are gonna do a blah, blah, blah. Come up with your idea right now." I'm like, "I'm just not that invested. It's not enough time for me to have an idea."

When explaining that she invited students to start thinking about their ideas three weeks before the start of their projects, Irene noted that this was prompted by her awareness of "how much time it takes a human being to come up with an idea." Reflecting on the importance of making space for learners to spend extended periods of time just talking through their ideas with each other, she made an analogy to her own creative work in sewing, noting that she spends long periods of time looking at examples and talking with others about what to do.

But in our conversations with her, despite her commitments and successes in the classroom, we also heard how Irene struggled to make time for students to develop ideas that were genuinely theirs and to make things that they cared about, given outside pressures. She was acutely conscious, for instance, of how the many demands on classroom time, and the AP curriculum in particular, impacted learners' creative processes. Due to the need to adhere to the preparation timeframe for AP exams, she sometimes had to interrupt students' work, derailing them when they were in the midst of constructing their projects. She lamented the necessity of doing so, even as she recognized value in the breadth of the curriculum. Irene was navigating a process Rinaldi described as the essence of teaching: "to constantly search for—without ever finding—a balance between rules and limitations (some of which are obviously indispensable) and the real emotion and passion of learning."[14]

Irene also sometimes felt a tension regarding the legibility of her practices to others, such as other teachers or her administrators, and the extent to which they would be able to see and understand the structure and deployment of time in her classroom. Reflecting on a class session that she had dedicated to brainstorming, she explained:

> Maybe today didn't look productive. Maybe if I got observed today they would have said, "What do the kids really do?" Sometimes I feel this internal pressure to put these deadlines and be like, "You have to know what your topic is, and make a plan, make a sketch." But when I stop and think about it, I'm like, "Yeah, even if they do have to sort of scramble a little bit more later, it's better if they're invested in the idea and that's the idea they want."

This challenge of legibility echoes the concern that Rinaldi named of schools becoming places of production rather than places of life. Even if we believe that time for dreaming and imagining is ultimately what is most meaningful for learners' engagement with ideas, it can look to others like learners are producing less, accomplishing less. This perception, and its concomitant pressure to conform, in turn, can make it difficult for us as teachers to hold onto the commitment that Irene has made to giving students more time. However, as teachers in the classroom as design studio, we can choose to advance an alternative approach. By responding resourcefully to practical structures and constraints, as well as resisting external perceptions and internal doubts, we can find ways, as Irene has, to make time for ideas, for creative process. In doing so, we foster the development of what Rinaldi envisioned: our students as whole human beings and our classrooms as places of life.

DO YOU THINK YOU KNOW HOW TO START?

In Benjamin's STEM class, his fifth graders have just started a multiweek *choice project*—a learning experience in which students choose a technology and a topic to explore with that technology. Some students revisit tools and techniques that are familiar to them, like creating a digital slideshow or constructing a diorama. But others take the opportunity to do something they've never done before.

"I want to make a motorized wheel that shows facts about the African wild dog," one fifth-grader tells Benjamin. "But I don't know how." Benjamin tilts his head thoughtfully and comments, "I don't know how, either." Then he asks, "Do you think you know how to start?"

The student is inspired by previous work the class has done using simple computers and motors, and imagines using those tools to enact his vision. As he starts building a prototype, he realizes that the motors the class has used previously won't work for this particular project; the motors move very quickly, too quickly for facts about the dog to be readable, and the motor can't be slowed down.

Seeing what his student is trying to create, Benjamin pulls out a set of motors from a different construction kit for the student to try. The student replaces the motors in his prototype and spends time tinkering with the programming of these new motors, experimenting with different speeds until he finds the ideal pace at which to display his facts.

When Benjamin shared this classroom experience with us, he emphasized the student's ownership over the project: "That was his idea. That's what he wanted to do." What Benjamin identified as powerful here was that the student had his own idea about what he wanted to create. And equally important, what the student wanted to create was something he had never done before and didn't entirely know how to enact, but that uncertainty did not prevent him from trying. Benjamin shared that this is his desire for every learner in his classroom: that they feel confident in their ideas.

Confidence is a complicated descriptor; it might be interpreted as certitude or fixedness or, pejoratively, as arrogance. For Benjamin, confidence means a conviction that one's ideas are worth pursuing, and a willingness to pursue them, absent certainty of the outcome. As he explained:

> I aspire to instill in my students a trait I have seen referred to as "creative confidence." For me, that means students pursuing their interests and ideas without fear of being wrong. It means that they are willing to take chances and to push their abilities in spite of their awareness that they may fail to accomplish what they are trying to do.

This is what we see in his student's work on the African wild dog project. The student has a vision, something that interests him and that he wants to create for his own reasons. But, he doesn't know how to realize it in practice. Undeterred, the student *tries*—he experiments with familiar and unfamiliar motors, he asks for advice from Benjamin, and he tinkers until he is successful.

The work of Eleanor Duckworth—Canadian-born scholar of education research, teacher, and student of psychologist Jean Piaget—helps us see how, for this student, making a motorized wheel showing facts about the African wild dog was a *wonderful idea,* and the process of figuring out how to investigate and realize that idea was a meaningful process of intellectual growth and development. In her 1972 essay "The Having of Wonderful Ideas," Duckworth wrestled with the legacy of Piaget and his ideas for work in the classroom. She saw limitations in how his stage-based theory of cognitive development was frequently used to either discourage teachers from introducing complex ideas to young learners or to unproductively focus teachers on purposefully moving learners from one stage to the next. She recognized the frustrations of teachers, feeling that this left them without ideas for how to meaningfully engage with and respond to children's own thinking in the moment.

Inspired in part by Piaget's less frequently acknowledged practices of listening to children and taking their ideas seriously, Duckworth concluded that it was not the specifics of a given idea on its own that makes it wonderful or not, but rather the meaning that it has for the learner and the role it plays in their own relationship to understanding the world around them. This is what Duckworth saw in her own research, related through a story of asking elementary school–aged children to put a group of straws in order from longest to shortest. The first two children she encountered completed the task easily, but with no interest or intellectual engagement in what they were doing. Then, she encountered Kevin who, before she had the opportunity to explain the task, excitedly told her that he had an idea for what to do with the straws, and proceeded to try putting them in order from longest to shortest. This proved much more difficult for him than for the other two students but he was deeply invested in the process and proud of the outcome. What made all the difference in the value of this learning experience was the meaning that putting the straws in order had for Kevin, the fact that it was his idea, and especially that he initially didn't know how to do it. As Duckworth explained:

> The having of wonderful ideas is what I consider the essence of intellectual development. And I consider it the essence of pedagogy to give Kevin the occasion to have his wonderful ideas and to let him feel good about himself for having them.[15]

Through the process of articulating his own idea for what he wanted to do and his own questions about how to do it, and persisting in figuring things out, Benjamin's student had the opportunity not only to create something of meaning to him and to learn how to do something he hadn't before, but also to believe in himself as someone who *could* have ideas and figure things out.

In addition to offering a conception of intellectual development as the having of wonderful ideas, of children developing their own ideas about the world and figuring out how to pursue them, Duckworth underscored the significance of schools and what they can provide to this process of development. She wrote that schools "can help to uncover parts of the world which children would not otherwise know how to tackle. Wonderful ideas build on other wonderful ideas. They are not had without content."[16] What we see in the work of Benjamin and the other teachers whose classrooms we studied are the remarkable ways in which teachers provide the supportive conditions for learners to have their own ideas, and develop the confidence to try them out. As Duckworth signaled in the preceding quote, part of this work has to do with content, with creating intellectually rich and stimulating environments in which learners are prompted to have ideas about things in the first place. Benjamin is helping students have experiences and develop expertise that they can then return to (such as the students who returned to familiar tools for this choice project) or build on and extend (such as the student featured in this vignette, who expanded his earlier experiences with motors to develop his rotating facts display). Benjamin is also providing the fifth graders with specific materials for experimentation in response to individual student interests, desires, and plans. On his own, Benjamin's student in the vignette may not have known about other motors, or that other motors might have slower spin rates, and thus would not have been able to use these tools and concepts in the service of his own creation.

But the supportive surround Benjamin is creating is also embedded in the culture and affective experience of his classroom, the element of pedagogy Duckworth identified as helping learners feel good about their ideas, and feel good about themselves for having them. Benjamin receives learners' own ideas with seriousness, and encourages a stance toward experimentation and trying that communicates his confidence in their ability to figure things out. This is evidenced by the inclusion of the choice project itself—the outcome of which is inherently uncertain—and by how he encourages his students as they tackle the unfamiliar:

> A lot of the kids, I'll hear them when they're brainstorming or talking to their partners or whatever. I'll be walking around and you can hear them talking. "I don't know if we can do that." Or "I don't know how to do that." And I try to encourage them, like, "Do you think you know how to start? Try!" Some of them will try. And then some of them, if they get frustrated, some of them will want to abandon it. I try to keep them working on it—that confidence to try it even if they're not sure it's going to work.

Benjamin described seeing a shift in his students over time, a change in how they relate to not knowing how to do something and the impact that has on their pursuit of their own ideas. Rather than abandoning their work in the face of uncertainty, they start to say, "I don't know how to do that, but I'll figure it out." This is the essence of the creative confidence Benjamin wants for his students, the essence of the culture of wonderful ideas that can flourish in the classroom as design studio. As Eleanor Duckworth wrote, "having confidence in one's ideas doesn't mean 'I know my ideas are right'; it means 'I am willing to try out my ideas.'"[17]

WHAT'S A GOOD THING THAT HAPPENED IN YOUR LIFE THIS WEEK?

Like many elementary classroom teachers, Karina spends considerable time and energy at the beginning of the year establishing a classroom culture through structures, routines, and expectations for how members of the learning community will interact with one another. She explicitly tells her third graders, "We are a supportive classroom culture." She invites them to practice engaging in productive discourse, sharing their ideas and respectfully agreeing and disagreeing, exploring multiple perspectives together. She holds both regular and impromptu class meetings, establishing shared norms of behavior and creating gentle reminders that learners use with one another when they are distracting each other from work or forgetting to be kind. Karina embodies this culture of concern and support in her own behavior, standing at the doorway each morning to greet each student individually as they come in, and gathering the class together at the end of the week to connect, asking, "What's a good thing that happened in your life this week?"

Karina believes that when learners feel safe and supported—with and by her, with and by their peers—they are willing to take the intellectual risks that accompany open-ended creation, able to let go of the fear of what might happen when things inevitably work out differently than expected. Students in her classroom are comfortable choosing to do things they don't know how to do—such as writing the code for a digital puzzle or recording a voice-over for an animated program—because they're confident that they will be able to figure it out over time with the help of their teacher and peers. Students who are still struggling with the mechanics of programming feel safe sharing their work with others. Sometimes when learners approach Karina with a question about how to do something in their program, another student nearby will say, "I know how to do that" and run over to offer help.

While Karina works hard to embed this safe and supportive culture in routines and practices that enable intellectual work to move forward, sometimes her commitment to the human beings in her classroom means stopping everything. One day in the spring, two students begin crying uncontrollably. Karina brings the class together for a meeting, asking everyone to sit and talk about what is going on. The students explain that they are experiencing especially difficult and painful things in their personal lives, prompting others in the class to share similar experiences. Seeing that these intense feelings need recognition and outlet within the classroom community, Karina suggests that they make a "kindness garden" and put encouraging notes there for one another. Rather than proceeding with their regularly scheduled work in language arts, the class spends the rest of the afternoon attending to one another's concerns and emotional needs through creating this special space in the classroom.

Through these routines and interactions—both planned and unplanned—Karina is responsive and attentive to the third graders in her room as complete human beings, with needs, experiences, and emotions that impact their learning in the classroom. Welcoming each student at the door, she acknowledges their individuality as they enter the learning space. This acknowledgment is carried through in rituals in which she asks them about their lives outside of school, and in moments when she halts the usual trajectory of the day for a necessary focus on feelings and experiences. She supports them in developing ways of talking with one another, disagreeing with one another, and helping one another that are respectful of difference and supportive of connection. The work of American philosopher and teacher Nel Noddings can help us see these multiple moves as acts of care—from Karina for her students, and as invitations of care for each other. Noddings's work is an argument for the centrality of care to the human experience, and thus its necessary (and often underrecognized) place in educational environments. As she wrote in her 1992 book *The Challenge to Care in Schools*:

> To care and be cared for are fundamental human needs. We all need to be cared for by other human beings. In infancy, illness, or old age, the need is urgent and pervasive; we need caregiving, and we need the special attitude of caring

that accompanies the best caregiving if we are to survive and be whole. But at every stage we need to be cared for in the sense that we need to be understood, received, respected, and recognized.[18]

Noddings's research and philosophy explored the relationship and interactions between those who give care and those who receive care, whom she referred to as the *carer* and the *cared-for*, respectively. In multiple works, Noddings described the actions of the teacher as carer, a conception with implications for how she understood the intersecting relationships of teacher, student, and subject matter. She called attention to the importance of the type of inquiring and listening that Karina does in her classroom, which are efforts to truly understand the learner and what they are thinking and feeling. As Noddings described in a 2012 article titled "The Caring Relation in Teaching":

> The attention of the carer is receptive. Its objective is to understand what the cared-for is experiencing—to hear and understand the needs expressed. From the perspective of care ethics, the teacher as carer is interested in the *expressed* needs of the cared-for, not simply the needs assumed by the school as an institution and the curriculum as a prescribed course of study.[19]

The distinction Noddings makes here between expressed needs and assumed needs is crucial. What is important about the specific incident Karina shared with us is that she listened to the words and actions of her students that communicated their distress, their inability to proceed with learning as it had been planned, and she responded with a decision to do something different, something out of the ordinary. While Karina shared her concern with us that an administrator walking in wouldn't necessarily have understood or supported that decision, her listening and her responsiveness to the expressed needs of her students are central to a care that enables self-directed learning in the classroom as design studio.

Noddings was concerned not only with individuals' own experiences of care in classrooms, but also with schools' commitment to helping all young people grow in their capacity to care for others. Seen through the lens of Noddings's work, Karina's approach is two-fold: she is modeling in her own behavior what it means to care for others; but also, in genuinely caring for her students, she is further enabling that development of a caring ethic. As Noddings explained, it is through being cared for ourselves that we are best able to care for others. Karina demonstrates care for her students, and we also see how her students express care toward each other.

We see how care enables learning in Karina's classroom, through the foregrounding of learners' responsibilities to and concern for one another. Karina asserted that helping students feel safe and supported and encouraging them to expand the boundaries of what they think is possible for themselves are mutually supportive aspirations, rather than conflicting ones. As she explained, "I think they go hand in hand. They're not going to push themselves if they don't already feel safe and secure in the classroom. And so you need to have one before you can have the other."

It is because the learners in her classroom feel cared about—by her, by their peers—that they are able to explore and make discoveries in their programming work. They are unafraid to try things even when uncertain of the outcome, because they know that their struggles or frustrations will be responded to with compassion and understanding. As Karina observed, "If you have that safe and supportive classroom as your foundation, you can challenge students and they feel safe to take risks, and they don't feel like kids are going to pick on them if they fail." In her work, Noddings recognized how a myopic focus on academic achievement and the culture of competition that often accompanies it can not only obscure needed attention to care but also "contribute to students' feeling that adults do not care for them."[20] In Karina's classroom, we see her inviting students into a fundamental orientation to learning in which others are not a measure to compare yourself against but rather a resource to enable you to do your best work.

When we asked Karina what she was most proud of in her work, she said:

> I think I'm most proud of seeing students working together to problem solve. This year, a lot of them were able to help each other instead of just relying on me. And that goes back to that kind of culture as well, with them feeling like they're in a safe environment and they can challenge themselves, but they also have supports around them.

The safe and supportive environment that Karina described tends to be more often associated with elementary school classrooms, where learners spend six hours a day with one another over the course of the school year, sharing their lives with each other, seeing one another's strengths and struggles across multiple dimensions and arenas. As Karina emphasized, the community in her classroom is one of learners who are deeply, fundamentally supportive of each other as they work to bring their ideas into the world—taking risks, trying things that don't work out, and continuing to grow. But the safety and support that make this possible need not be exclusive to elementary classrooms; as we see across this collection of classroom stories, teachers at any grade level can work to foster this type of caring environment. In doing so, they establish a powerful foundation for self-directed learning in their classrooms.

WHAT'S INTERESTING ABOUT THIS?

For the past several years, Janet has invited her sixth-grade students into an interdisciplinary exploration of geoscience and computer science; students each choose a geological process and then program a digital animation or simulation of that process. As she was preparing to launch this year's exploration, she remembered that students' projects from last year, while good, weren't especially different from each other and, notably, not especially different from the example she had shown them for inspiration. She wondered whether showing students a range of projects—differing in their topics, their technical complexity, and their aesthetic qualities—might lead to more personalized outcomes.

This year, Janet begins the project by sharing several examples, created by students from previous years, to inspire her current students' sense of creative possibilities. Janet has selected three projects to share: one that is beautiful, but not scientifically accurate; one that is accurate, but not engaging to interact with; and one that lacks detail. She encourages her students to have their own thoughts and opinions about the examples, asking a series of questions about each project: "What's interesting about this? What do you find functional about it as a scientist? What do you find aesthetically pleasing about it as an artist? What would you change?" With these questions as a starting place, the group discusses each of the examples, appreciating the strengths and making suggestions for possible revisions.

Following this opening examination of examples, students start their own projects. Janet sees a range of projects being developed, each one representative of her students' unique personalities and styles. One student, with an interest in writing and drama, produces a project in which she anthropomorphizes a sediment fragment, having it narrate its journey. Another student, who is passionate about illustration, wants to capture how the fossil record is layered onto rocks and figures out how to create multiple layers of decomposition on top of a background. One student who had never coded before makes a simple and elegant animation of a rock eroding over time. Another student, who has prior technical experience, focuses on the process of animating labels for different geological elements.

Mitchel Resnick, the LEGO Papert Professor of Learning Research at the MIT Media Lab, has dedicated his life to designing learning experiences and tools that enable people to think and act creatively—to imagine possibilities, express themselves, and create things they care about. One of his most notable projects was the development of Scratch, a visual, blocks-based programming language accompanied by an online community in which young people are able to share their creations with others. While other programming environments had been developed for young learners—some available for decades prior to Scratch, such as the Logo programming language developed by Resnick's mentor Seymour Papert—having an online space for learners to share their creations represented a novel contribution and serves as an incredible catalog of children's imaginations. Writing about the design of Scratch in a 2009 article for *Communications of the ACM*, a few years after Scratch's launch, Resnick described the significance of this online space for young creators:

> For many Scratchers, the opportunity to put their projects in front of a large audience—and receive feedback and advice from other Scratchers—is strong motivation. The large library of projects on the site also serves as inspiration. By exploring projects there, Scratchers get ideas for new projects and learn new programming techniques. Marvin Minsky once said that Logo had a great grammar but not much literature. Whereas young writers are often inspired by reading great works of literature, there was no analogous library of great Logo projects to inspire young programmers. The Scratch Web site is the beginning of a "literature" for Scratch.[21]

On a smaller scale, we see the power of inspiration through examples in Janet's classroom. Janet described to us the shift she made in her classroom practice, sharing examples to open up, rather than close off, creative possibilities. As she explained, she saw how her past strategy of giving a single, idealized example could be "the benchmark that limited what kids thought they should or could do with the project." Janet said her new approach led to visible changes in students' work and how they seemed to feel about their creations:

Looking at "non-perfect" examples was helpful in that students saw a variety of ideas, but not one certain model of how it is supposed to be done. Sometimes giving students models that are "perfect" makes the work seem impossible and unattainable. This method seemed to support the students feeling more confident in initiating the project—and we seem to have more variety and creative expression in our final products.

There are several dimensions to the shift that Janet makes here. First, she is showing multiple examples, rather than a single one, highlighting a range of approaches to the project. Second, she is curating the examples to include ones that are, as she describes, intentionally imperfect, encouraging a mindset of revision with her learners. Finally, Janet asks her students a set of four questions to help them see the examples as potentially helpful to their own creative work. Her first question—"What's interesting to you?"—communicates to students that it is what they think of the examples that is important, that their perspective, their own ideas about things, are central in this process. Her last question—"What would you change?"—is Janet's way of helping students understand that examples aren't precious. Examples are things to think with, not things to replicate, or even necessarily aspire to. Janet invites students to think about these changes through the dual lenses of scientist and artist that so uniquely characterize her classroom, encouraging them to inhabit and experiment with these identities.

In his 2017 book *Lifelong Kindergarten*, Resnick elaborated on this theme, describing the importance of examples to the creative process, particularly when getting started with a new endeavor.

A blank page, a blank canvas, and a blank screen can be intimidating. A collection of examples can help spark the imagination. When we run Scratch workshops, we always start by showing sample projects—to give a sense of what's possible (inspirational projects) and to provide ideas on how to get started (starter projects). We show a diverse range of projects, in hopes of connecting with the interests and passions of workshop participants.[22]

This passage illuminates the delicate and nuanced work at play in Janet's thoughtful, purposeful deployment of examples to support students' creative work. Sometimes, motivated by worries we might have as teachers about crowding out students' own ideas and creative possibilities, we restrict access to examples. At other times, concerned that students might not have sufficient support or direction, we are overly prescriptive with examples. Navigating these two extremes, Janet judiciously offers students examples as supportive avenues into the work—ideas of what to do, ideas of where to start—in ways that expand, rather than preclude, creative possibilities.

We see the impact of Janet's curation process in the wide variety of projects that her students create. In Janet's classroom, one student focuses much more on technical labeling and documentation, while another uses the project to express an interest in dramatic narrative. They are using the programming environment for different purposes and at different levels of sophistication, making use of different features and functions. Janet explained that one of the examples she chose to show was a very simple animation of a rock eroding over time, to show students that something simple could be both scientifically accurate and beautiful. But when one of her students was interested in illustrating how the fossil record is layered into rocks, he realized he needed to learn a more complicated technique and Janet worked with him to create a series of images that would change over time.

Students in her class are not only pursuing topics that are interesting to them; they are pursuing those topics in ways that are meaningful and appropriate for them. Citing his mentor Seymour Papert,[23] Resnick offered the metaphor of *low floors, high ceilings, and wide walls* to describe a learning activity or technology that makes it easy to begin, supports varying degrees of technical and aesthetic complexity, and invites a range of approaches in what students make and in how they make it. As he explained, "Children differ from one another not only in their interests and passions, but also in the ways they play and learn. If we want to help all children develop as creative thinkers, we need to support all types of play styles and learning styles."[24]

Resnick observed that many students are turned off from math and science precisely because those disciplines are not taught in ways that enable learners to see themselves in the work, to create things they care about in ways that work for them. Here, Janet has crafted a classroom as design studio experience with a very specific disciplinary focus and with very clear content boundaries, all while creating space for individual expression in the context of a project. Her commitment to enabling students' deep understanding of geological processes is intertwined with her commitment to enabling them to develop and express their own ideas, all beginning with a critical and reflective stance toward inspiration.

HOW COULD YOU USE THIS FOR YOUR OWN IDEAS?

When a group of third graders enters Betsy's elementary STEAM lab, they encounter books spread on tables throughout the room. The books are fairy tales and folktales, as many different ones as she could find at both the school and local libraries. Betsy invites her students to spend time exploring the different stories. She explains their new project: creating a mechanical device that helps a character from one of the stories. She encourages them to think expansively about what they might do, reminding them that they can design for any of the characters, the heroes or the villains, because "bad guys also have problems that need solving." Excited about this opportunity to respond in their own way to an existing story, one student exclaims, "What? I can help the wolf!?!"

As students focus on the character they want to help and begin imagining the details of the character's story, they start creating their mechanical devices using programmable blocks and motors. In support of their construction work, Betsy introduces her students to an online resource library that shows examples of possible constructions using the blocks and motors and how to start building them. She encourages them to spend time playing around with the materials and resources, as part of the process of getting a sense of what they might want to do.

Betsy circulates among the students as they work, asking them questions about the examples in the library such as, "What do you like and not like? What ideas does this give you? How could you use this for your own ideas?" Students explore and make discoveries, remarking, "Ah-ha, that's how that works!" Some students start with the idea of building a car but pivot to creating an alarm system, inspired by the car's wheels to use a rotating component. Other students are excited by the concept of a motion sensor but modify the design so that it is disguised as a mailbox. One team of students imagines creating a lift to help characters from "Jack and the Beanstalk," while another creates a trap on top of a large house from "The Three Little Pigs."

Through both the conceptual and technical dimensions of this project, Betsy invites her students to think about how they can repurpose, reuse, reinterpret, and remix existing elements in the service of their own creations. She explained to us that the impetus for this particular project was a desire for students to have opportunities to express themselves and feel ownership over their learning. This was partly inspired by a conversation she had with the district's high school computer science teachers who said they preferred students come to class with "a passion for learning, and enthusiasm," as Betsy put it, over having specific pieces of knowledge, like what a "loop" is. Betsy described how she saw students responding to opportunities for expression: "It's their own idea, and they love it, they really get into being able to express their idea creatively with the build." But central to this project is the way in which such expression is enabled and enriched by engagement with existing material. When Betsy asks her students, "How can you use this for your own ideas?," she is inviting learners to see how the ideas of others—the collection of fairy tales, the library of possible mechanical creations—can be used to help them create something of their own.

This was not the first time that Betsy used this project. In earlier years, she had students design mechanical devices using the same constructive materials, but she did not introduce them to the resource library. Her previous approach was grounded in the widespread idea that students would learn more by having to do everything themselves, and a response to the worry that giving them a model with which to begin would limit them creatively, closing off an opportunity for them to formulate their own ideas as they built technical competency. But Betsy observed that students really struggled with understanding how to attach the motors and integrate them into something that could actually move, and that these difficulties with the underlying technical dimensions seemed to impede both the development of students' ideas for what they might want to build and their ability to move forward in their understanding.

When Betsy introduced the resource library and helped frame its utility for learners as being in the service of their own ideas, it opened up their creative imaginations. Ultimately, she felt that this experience—encountering scaffolded starting points, figuring out how to build upon them, and learning to implement their own designs—was important in helping learners see themselves as people capable of creation.

> I think what it helped solidify for the kids is a level of confidence. That they did know enough about the coding and the engineering. That they could create something themselves and make it the idea that they had as a team or as an individual. That they could make it come to life. So I think it was kind of like that reaffirmation and confirmation for the students that this is something they can do.

When Betsy asked the third graders to reflect on their learning experiences over the year and how they thought they had grown, many articulated that they felt more capable of creativity and creative endeavors than they had before. And, because they were able to actually make things and were highly invested in figuring out how to realize their visions, they were also able to achieve more on the technical side than students in previous years.

In their book *Hanging Out, Messing Around, and Geeking Out,* originally published in 2009, cultural anthropologist Mizuko Ito and her colleagues explored how young people engage with new media, recognizing the centrality of the concept and practices of remixing (an approach to creating new content by modifying and combining existing content) to emerging cultures of digital and online creative production. As happened with Betsy's students' reimagining of fairy-tale characters, the authors observed that when young people curate images and sounds and integrate them into their online profiles, or when they create animated videos using existing genre conventions and characters, they are saying something about themselves, about who they are and what is important to them. As the authors wrote:

> Our understanding of what constitutes creative production includes imaginative and expressive forms that are also shaped by kids' individual choices and available media. The influx of digital media into everyday life is reshaping these understandings, particularly our assumptions about the relation between media production and consumption. Media theorists have argued for decades that media "consumption" is not a passive act and that viewers and readers actively shape cultural meanings.[25]

Ito and colleagues noted that remix practices are not always seen as legitimate forms of either expression or learning. They can be dismissed as lesser compared to creating something entirely on your own—or seen as a way of avoiding work. Arguing to the contrary, Ito and colleagues' extensive ethnographic research demonstrated how young people's access to others and others' work (both work by peers and those more distant, in age or expertise) helps young people to figure out their own ideas, to develop their own sense of self, and to understand their own capacities.

Betsy noted that it was necessary to allocate more time for the project than she had in the past in order for students to be able to explore existing materials as they figured out their own ideas. She wanted her students to have time to look through things in an unhurried manner, to figure out what they liked and didn't like, and then to reflect on what they wanted to do. She wanted time for learners to "mess around productively." As suggested by her use of "productively" as a qualifier, Betsy wrestled with justifying the time for "messing around" to others (both adults and children); the term itself carries connotations that can seem antithetical to (or at least distracting from) the serious business of learning. However, Ito and colleagues showed how young people's experiences of messing around—following interests where they lead, finding things, exploring media without an otherwise specific or targeted goal in mind—can help to blur "the boundary between 'casual' and social media production and 'serious' media production."[26] They found that having time for messing around can help young people define themselves and what they are interested in more clearly, sometimes prompting them to pursue greater technical competencies and to seek out support in trying to create things that reflect the ideas they have developed.

Hanging Out, Messing Around, and Geeking Out was an intervention in cultural understandings of what it means to learn and make things. As the authors wrote:

> The negotiations among kids, parents, educators, and technologists over the shape of youth online participation is also a site of struggle over what counts as legitimate forms of learning and literacy. Any discussion of learning and literacy is unavoidably normative. What counts as learning and literacy is a question of collective values, values that are constantly being contested and negotiated among different social groups. Periods of cultural and technological flux open

up new areas of debate about what should count as part of our common culture and literacy and what are appropriate ways for young people to participate in these new cultural forms.[27]

Ito and colleagues were speaking to both parents and educators in urging them to recognize the value of young people's explorations with new media, including the remix practices described here, for helping young people to develop and express a sense of self, engage with ideas, build technical competencies, and see themselves as people capable of creation—all core goals of the classroom as design studio. In arguing for the legitimacy of these explorations and noting their prevalence in out-of-school learning experiences, the authors were not saying that such forms of learning could not happen in schools: rather, they were calling attention to what might be lost when such experiences are dismissed out of hand as superficial or disconnected from what is most meaningful in content learning and creative expression. Betsy does not need to be convinced of the legitimacy of remix practices for learning—either for developing ideas or for building technical capacity—and her project exemplifies how these practices can be integrated into school-based learning experiences. Instead, she sees her work as inviting her students to see the value of messing around and remixing, of asking themselves, "How could you use this for your own ideas?"

WHAT DO YOU WANT TO DO?

Jess has organized her classroom with the aim of helping her elementary students feel comfortable physically, socially, and intellectually—able to express themselves, be themselves, and follow their instincts as they work alongside each other. There are rows of computers where students can work independently, but easily peek over at what a neighbor is working on. There is a carpet at the front of the room where the class assembles for group meetings. She has covered all of the overhead lights in the room with blue paper, and gently illuminates the space with lamps she has collected over the years.

Jess's fourth graders have been working on coding digital animation projects for a few weeks. She has her own ideas about what might be productive for students at this moment in the creative process, such as opportunities to get feedback on their work from peers or to look at other projects for inspiration. Jess suspects that some students might just need a break, engaging in a different activity after so much coding. She is interested in what her learners think they need.

At the beginning of today's class, the students gather on the carpet at the front of the classroom. Jess welcomes them warmly and then gestures to a list on the whiteboard at the front of the room. "You have three choices for what you can do with your time today," she says. "If you're ready for feedback, you can participate in a gallery walk. If you're not ready for feedback, you can work on your project. And if you feel maxed out on coding, you can practice your typing. What do you want to do?"

Students take different amounts of time to declare their decisions. Some students rush up to the board right away and add their names and their plans for the session. Others sit for a bit to consider the options. A few students go over to Jess, wanting to talk through their thinking before making a choice. Students who are interested in receiving feedback move toward their computers. They pull up their projects-in-progress and put a class-designed feedback form in front of their computers to solicit ideas and reactions from the small groups of students gathering around to look at what they've done. Students who want time to work on their own project settle in, putting on headphones and turning their full attention to coding. And a few others, welcoming the opportunity Jess has created for a change of pace, take a break from programming to try a new typing program.

The practice Jess employs here may seem simple or straightforward: she presents students with choices about what to work on in a given class period and asks students what they want to do. But while the idea of choice in the classroom is not new, it is not always motivated by the same values. Too often choice is advocated for and employed absent an underlying examination of the purpose it serves. For Jess, to offer students choice is not a superficial practice; choice is not being used as a motivational gimmick or a reward. Instead, it reflects her deeply held commitment to designing learning experiences that recognize, value, and support learners' own ideas about what they want to do and how they want to do it, key attributes of the classroom as design studio. The respect that Jess offers her students is evidenced by how she encourages them to make choices for themselves and how she honors their individual decisions—and is further underscored by the seriousness with which she speaks to them and listens to them. When Jess talked to us about how she understood classroom practice that was in the service of learners' expressive and creative instincts, she explained that it "emerges as a result of consistently and consciously embracing a way of being and doing that is about unleashing freedom."

Alongside the expression of this aspiration, though, Jess was quick to acknowledge its accompanying complexity in practice. The process of "unleashing freedom" can be difficult for both her and the students. Jess related an incident where one of the fourth graders working on a coding project hadn't been progressing in the work due to a mundane logistical challenge. The student hadn't spoken up. When Jess finally noticed the student was struggling, she was upset that she hadn't noticed sooner.

Despite occasional moments where students might not necessarily be working in ways that are most productive for them, Jess still values creating the space for them to choose, to not be held back by what she, as the teacher, might think is best for them. As she explained:

> Providing enough of a structure but still giving them opportunities to explore is really a very hard and careful balance. Because I don't want to ever be domineering. I'd rather err on the side that they might feel a little bit like they're floundering rather than, "Well, Jess wants it this way." I think it's still better off. The floundering will happen, but then the confidence increases. And then the floundering decreases.

In her actions and her descriptions, Jess threads together three powerful ideas: (1) learners have enormous capability to make decisions about their learning; (2) decision-making processes can be unfamiliar and challenging; and (3) freedom and choice can be supported through classroom design decisions.

That freedom doesn't just *happen* is an idea that English sociologist Anthony Giddens advanced with structuration theory, which engages a similar interleaving of the ideas of agency and structure. First, Giddens frames agency as fundamental to our human experience. "To be a human being," he wrote, "is to be a purposive agent."[28] Giddens connected his concept of agency to the power of consequential decision-making, such as we see in Jess's classroom. As he wrote in his 1984 book *The Constitution of Society*:

> To be able to "act otherwise" means being able to intervene in the world, or to refrain from such intervention, with the effect of influencing a specific process or state of affairs. This presumes that to be an agent is to be able to deploy (chronically, in the flow of daily life) a range of causal powers, including that of influencing those deployed by others. Action depends upon the capability of the individual to "make a difference" to a pre-existing state of affairs or course of events. An agent ceases to be such if he or she loses the capability to "make a difference," that is, to exercise some sort of power.[29]

The actions and interventions that Jess's students are making are in the service of their own learning, their own sense of what is important to that process and what they are trying to do. Jess is enabling them to exercise the power that Giddens named, the power to make a difference, because the choices she presents them with are genuine, without a predetermined outcome, and consequential to their work.

Giddens argued that our ability—or inability—to exercise that agency is shaped by a variety of individual, social, and material structures. While agency and structure may seem fundamentally incompatible, Giddens helps us see how they are mutually constitutive, with structures serving to make our actions possible or not. We draw upon the existing social surround in acting, and in doing so we generate the social surround that is available to act within and upon.

> The constitution of agents and structures are not two independently given sets of phenomena, a dualism, but represent a duality. According to the notion of the duality of structure, the structural properties of social systems are both medium and outcome of the practices they recursively organize. Structure is not "external" to individuals: as memory traces, and as instantiated in social practices, it is in a certain sense more "internal" than exterior to their activities. . . . Structure is not to be equated with constraint but is always both constraining and enabling.[30]

It is the final note here, that structure is always both constraining and enabling, that especially illuminates the purposeful design of Jess's classroom, the work she is doing to enable the experience of learner freedom she so deeply values. She is thoughtful about when she introduces this opportunity for choice: far enough along in the project that students have some sense of how things are going for themselves, and perhaps are also in need of a break. She helps to frame the meaning of the choices learners might be making, offering the language of being "ready for feedback" or "maxed out on coding," language that might help learners better recognize and advocate for their own needs in the future.

In the world of education, we seem to often have a hard time holding on to the nuance of this relationship between agency and structure, which Giddens offered in response to the twin pitfalls he perceived in other sociological theory: not taking the capacity and power of agents seriously enough and not taking the influence and meaning of structures seriously enough. In our worry that young people will not be able to determine for themselves what is meaningful and productive for their learning, we limit the scope and substance of the decisions they make in classrooms, and thus the occasions for their growth and development. And in our worry that we are then denying them necessary opportunities for expression and individuation, we attempt to throw off all constraints and supports, leaving them adrift. Finding ways to introduce structure into the classroom such that it enables (rather than constrains) learner agency and choice—fundamentally, in Jess's words, such that it "unleashes freedom"—is an essential task for the educator in the classroom as design studio. With every act, with every invitation, with every utterance, we must bring continuous attention and curiosity to how those manifestations of structure in the classroom are advancing the broader project of learner freedom.

DO YOU WANT TO MAKE ANY CHANGES?

On a sunny day in April, the first graders in elementary technology teacher Jenny's classroom gather on a rug at the front of the room. Jenny explains to her students that today they will be programming robots, entering special instructions called *commands* to help their robots navigate through a maze, telling their robots how quickly to move and in what direction. She explains that without these commands the robots won't know what to do. She encourages her students to embrace the process, especially when, unavoidably, things will not work. She asks them what they've learned to call a mistake in technology class, to which the students enthusiastically reply in chorus: "A bug!" Jenny reassures them, "We can always fix bugs."

Students begin to work in groups programming their robots, as Jenny circulates throughout the room. She approaches a group that is having difficulty getting their robot to follow the maze, and remarks, "So we have a little bug in our program." She asks the group what they might want to do differently. The students think for a moment, and then decide to try using a command that will turn the robot right instead of left.

Toward the end of class, Jenny has the class gather on the rug and asks one student to demonstrate the programming that she has figured out. The student takes a few moments to enter her series of commands, and then presses a button to have the robot start moving through the maze. The class watches as the robot heads in the wrong direction, ending up beyond the path's boundaries. Jenny asks the student, "Do you want to make any changes?" Jenny gives the student time to revise her program and fix the bug, reminding her that the class is there for support if she needs it. Many students on the rug offer ideas of what she could do, suggesting different directions and adjustments to the commands. The student listens, and then, with a revised plan in mind, reprograms the robot. She runs the program again, and the robot successfully navigates the maze.

In her classroom, Jenny invites young learners to think and act like programmers. Jenny talks with her students about the inevitable presence of mistakes, or *bugs*, in programming work. She explains that bugs are a necessary and expected aspect of this work, as the students try out their programs, see if they work, and try something else if they don't. She encourages students to be persistent: "When we have bugs in our system, we never give up. We just keep trying." The interaction with the student who demonstrated her program embodies Jenny's commitment to supporting her students as programmers. There is no anxiety on the part of Jenny or the students that things have not initially worked out as intended. The question Jenny asks the student—"Do you want to make any changes?"—is an appeal to the student's own decision-making and judgment as a programmer. This is an opportunity for the student to decide what to do next, to figure out for herself how to fix her program, supported by a community of other novice programmers.

In their 1991 book *Situated Learning: Legitimate Peripheral Participation*, American social anthropologist Jean Lave and Swiss learning theorist Etienne Wenger argued that moments like these are essential to the process of learning. Lave and Wenger's work is centered on the idea that learning happens when people new to a field or activity (whom they refer to as *newcomers*) have the opportunity to actually engage in that activity, with the support of people who themselves have experience and knowledge. The significance of their argument for our understanding of learning comes in their assertion that we do not learn *in order to do* the work; we learn *by doing* the work. As they wrote, "engaging in practice, rather than being its object, may well be a *condition* for the effectiveness of learning."[31] From this perspective, we don't learn programming by being told about programming, we learn programming by doing the actual work of programming, in situations that have been structured to account for our developing knowledge and skills and to provide the kinds of supports and accessible entry points into the work that we need as beginning programmers. It is precisely this type of experience, which Lave and Wenger called *legitimate peripheral participation*, that Jenny creates for her students.

Lave and Wenger underscored the role of identity in learning. Learning how to engage in a practice means coming to see oneself as a member of a community that engages in that practice. One of the central mechanisms through which this happens is how newcomers learn to talk about the practice, learn the language of the community. Lave and Wenger noted the significance of language—how important it is for learners to have opportunities to use the formal language of the community's work, such as the "bugs" and "commands" and "programs" vocabulary that we see Jenny using with her students. As Lave and Wenger wrote, "For newcomers then the purpose is not to learn *from* talk as a substitute for legitimate peripheral participation; it is to learn *to* talk as a key to legitimate peripheral participation."[32]

Through her use of talk, her interactions with learners, and the activities she invites them into, Jenny is dismantling two of the barriers to having these kinds of experiences that Lave and Wenger noted often exist within traditional schooling. First, Jenny is communicating that the actual work of programming is going on in the classroom, rather than the school curriculum differing from what programmers do. Second, she is pushing back against the traditional authority structures that can exist between teacher and student. Like other teachers in the classroom as design studio, Jenny is open to and excited about the ideas that learners themselves bring, in their expressions of individuality. She talked about students who were "showing me new things I've never even tested out before," and remarked, "I'm learning things from them, they're learning things from me, and I think it can go both ways."

But this excitement about learners' own ideas and practices does not come at the expense of structuring the work to recognize the particular position of newcomers, giving them ways to meaningfully engage in the work as they are developing knowledge and competency. Jenny is not putting a six-year-old in front of a computer, asking them to write a program, and walking away. Rather, she is thoughtfully offering structure and guidance, inviting them to build upon their nascent experiences of coding to do something real—to make a robot move—and helping them develop modes of understanding and action when, like professional programmers, things don't work out as intended. This is an important element of Lave and Wenger's conceptualization of learning, the *peripherality* of legitimate peripheral participation. While the authors used this word to indicate a difference between how you can do the work when you are a beginner and how you can do the work when you are more experienced, they make clear that "peripheral" is not a deficit position, but an opportunity. As they wrote: "In our usage, *peripherality* is a *positive* term, whose most salient conceptual antonyms are *unrelatedness* or *irrelevance* to on-going activity. The partial participation of newcomers is by no means 'disconnected' from the practice of interest."[33]

By offering them opportunities to program robots, Jenny is helping her students engage in the practice of interest. They are participating in meaningful opportunities to learn. But their participation is also supported through the forms of thinking she makes visible to them in her talk, and through her decisions about when to intervene with a question to prompt their thinking and when to step back to let them work through bugs on their own. In the classroom as design studio, taking learners seriously as participants in the work of creation involves connecting them with structures and supports necessary for the work of creating, for the work of becoming and being creators.

WOULD YOU LIKE TO STAY AND CODE WITH US THIS MORNING?

One morning in February, a group of first graders enters Kara's library media center. Kara explains that the students will have an opportunity to try out a programming environment designed for young children, telling them that with the tool, "You can make worlds however you want." Kara demonstrates some of the basics of the application, naming a subset of tools in the interface and showing them how to create a new background. The students are so excited to get started that, before they have even returned to their seats, they are beginning to work on the tablets in their hands—dragging visual code elements into their workspaces and changing the color of objects on the screen.

After watching the introduction from Kara, Diane, the students' classroom teacher, moves to leave the library media center. She is not typically present when the students are doing their work with Kara. But today Kara invites Diane to explore alongside her students. Kara asks, "Would you like to stay and code with us this morning?" Diane is appreciative of the invitation but hesitates, slightly uncertain of what it means to "stay and code." Some of her students pick up on the hesitation and guide Diane to a nearby table. They patiently show her how to open the app and start her own project.

Questions emerge as both students and their teacher work to figure out how to code the worlds and characters they are creating. One student wants to use a motion block to prompt a graphical element (commonly referred to as a *sprite*) to move a specific number of steps, and asks Kara, "How do I change the number?" Kara validates the value of the question, noting, "You know what? Your teacher just asked me how to do that, too!" and encourages them to continue experimenting and see if they can figure it out together. One student is able to change the color of an existing sprite and exclaims enthusiastically, "Oh, snap!"

Another girl clicks around as she figures out how to change elements in her background image. When things don't work out as she wants, she simply tries again with a different strategy. Diane sits among the students as a fellow learner, focused on expressing her ideas in a medium she hasn't used before. When she observes Diane experiencing a moment of struggle, Kara warmly remarks to her, "I like how genuinely confused you look!"

Eventually, the class period comes to a close. Students reluctantly put away their materials, finding it difficult to let go of the excitement generated by their explorations and creations. Diane shares their feelings of pride and satisfaction in working through challenges to make something she cares about. As she gets up from the table she declares, "That was the best thing I ever made in my whole life!"

In this class period, Kara invites her fellow educator Diane to experience the power of creation within community that characterizes the classroom as design studio. Diane is encouraged to have an idea and to explore the communication of that idea in a new medium, experiencing confusion and challenge, having questions along the way, and ultimately feeling good about having made something of her own. Kara notices Diane as she works, validating her experiences of not knowing and confusion by letting them stand and not jumping in to close them off, communicating that such experiences are necessary to the learning process. Diane works alongside her students. This is an opportunity for them to see her as a fellow learner—to see her struggling and not knowing—as well as an opportunity to help her, to make her feel more secure and confident, and thus gain greater confidence in their own powers of creation and problem-solving.

For students to have experiences of meaningful, open-ended creation, their teachers must have the same. Focusing on teachers as learners as a way of supporting their understanding of children as learners was one of the core principles of a 1978 seminar for working elementary teachers organized by educational researchers Jeanne Bamberger, Eleanor Duckworth, and Magdalene Lampert, which they titled "An Experiment in Teacher Development." Duckworth and Lampert had themselves been teachers, and all three researchers went on to make foundational contributions in the fields of music education, science education, and math education, respectively. Over the course of two years, the teachers who participated in the seminar engaged in open-ended, constructivist learning experiences for themselves (for example, observing the moon, using resonator bells, and building ramps) and discussed, in depth, the work they were doing with the students in their classrooms. In articulating the power of this experience the authors wrote:

> At one level, the teachers are learning about the moon, about making melodies, about long division, about measuring time. At this level, the primary experience is watching the moon, building tunes with the bells, and pertinent fields of knowledge can be thought of as astronomy, music, mathematics, and so on. At another level, the teachers are learning about learning. At this level, the primary experience is watching people learning—themselves, each other, and children—and the pertinent field of knowledge can be thought of as psychology. . . . Just as it seems clear to us—and the data confirms this—that the math, science, musical knowledge that people construct for themselves over time is more accessible to them than knowledge that they "receive" formally, so it seems clear to us that the same must hold true of knowledge about learning. That is, rather than being taught about psychology (rather than being taught about music theory), what needs to be done is to provide experiences that challenge teachers' knowledge about learning. Just like experiences which challenge their knowledge about math or science, these can push them to think about it more deeply, to take into account features they might have missed, and so on.[34]

When Bamberger, Duckworth, and Lampert originally designed the seminar, they had planned to present the teachers with the core principles of cognitive psychology, particularly the work of Jean Piaget, to help them develop new ways of understanding their work and its significance. But what the authors found was that the kinds of questions and ideas they might have posed as researchers were formulated by the teachers themselves when they had opportunities to participate in generative intellectual tasks and reflect on their experiences. The participating teachers learned about learning by being learners.

Bamberger and her colleagues found that one of the most significant changes in teachers through participation in the seminar was a shift toward seeing themselves as people capable of generating knowledge and figuring things out, a lessening of expectation that "answers" would be provided by external sources. While working with Eleanor Duckworth on elementary arithmetic, some of the teachers realized that they had their own methods for doing long division, but that they had been made to feel through their own experiences of schooling that those methods were wrong or bad. Embracing their own approaches, seeing them as something worth valuing and attending to, led to a shift in how the teachers related to their students' mathematical work. The teachers expressed to the researchers a new conviction to take seriously students' own strategies for approaching problems, along with a desire to understand the thinking behind those approaches. As the researchers wrote:

> The teachers learned both to question and to trust their own experience as learners; and as a result, in their work with children, they shifted from seeking and valuing "right answers" to valuing the capacity to seek out ways in which what a child says or does makes sense to himself and to others.[35]

Part of the experience of the seminar was them reclaiming, to themselves, their own ideas and their own ways of doing things.

For this to happen, teachers must believe in themselves as people with ideas to be taken seriously. This is the experience that Kara creates for Diane by inviting her to stay and code that morning. Through creating a project of her own design and working through the challenges that arise, Diane has the opportunity to see herself as she sees her students: as someone with ideas and capacity to realize those ideas. Yet such an experience can be as disconcerting as it is powerful. Kara often used the word "bravery" when speaking about her students' reactions to opportunities to explore, experiment, and create, noting that many would express concern to her about whether they were "doing it right." She would encourage them to trust themselves and their ideas, telling them in response, "I want you to try this, to have fun. I want you to learn how to use this particular app. Today's all about exploring and finding out how to use it." Later, in reflecting on her own perspective as a teacher, she mentioned her own questions and uncertainty about this approach to learning. Kara sometimes wrestled with whether she could really trust that meaningful learning would result from these more exploratory and open-ended experiences. Noting the parallels between her own uncertainty and her students' uncertainty, she said, "I need to take my own advice and be a little braver about letting them attempt."

Bravery is required to trust in your own ideas, to be willing to pursue them without certainty regarding the outcome; it is a bravery demanded of both learners and teachers in the classroom as design studio. There are practical reasons why others in Diane's situation might not have been able to accept Kara's invitation to stay and code, including myriad other forms of work (planning and preparation, contact with families, analysis of assessment data, writing of progress reports) that classroom teachers often do when their students are with a specialist like Kara. There can also be something unnerving about putting yourself in the position of learner, in revealing what you don't know, not only to your students, but to other adults. The designers of "An Experiment in Teacher Development" noted the bravery that comes with plunging into open-ended creation, and the vulnerability, but ultimate power, involved in engaging with other teachers around that work. As they wrote of the teachers:

> They became supportive of one another's confusions and fears, and in doing so, the participants were able to break through the isolation that they, like most teachers, experience: They discovered that they had shared puzzles, feelings of success and lack of it, and sometimes deep doubts about themselves as teachers and even about "school" as an enterprise. Finally, the participants learned <u>with</u> one another to face risks—the risks, for instance, of open-ended activities such as we asked them to participate in and the risks of exposing their various beliefs and ideas to scrutiny—their own as well as each other's.[36]

CAN YOU HELP US LEARN?

At a recent STEM institute for K–12 educators where she had an experience with a visual programming tool, elementary technology teacher Andrea was excited about the learning possibilities for her students. She went home and continued to explore on her own. After several days of playing around with the tool and making a variety of projects, she couldn't wait to introduce the tool to her class.

After showing her students some of the projects she had made, her students start creating animations with the tool, experimenting with different features and bringing their ideas and interests to life. One student figures out how to record sound and integrate it into the animation. His eyes lighting up, he tells Andrea, "I just thought it'd be cool!" Her student is so excited about his animation that he starts working on other animations with the tool at home. He asks Andrea if she would like to see the other projects he has made.

Thinking ahead to the next semester with this class, Andrea imagines moving from digital creations to robotics. She acquires a set of educational robots to use in the classroom; it comes with a guide, but Andrea wishes she had access to a more structured introduction or to others with greater expertise. Even though she's excited about the robots, she finds herself unable to figure out enough on her own to use them with the students.

Serendipitously, two students arrive at her classroom for an after-school tech club and excitedly run over to the robotics kits. "This is so cool," they say, "We've used these before!" Andrea responds, "Really? Can you help us learn?" The two students smile and reply, "We've got this." Over several weeks, these two students help tech club members and Andrea experiment with and learn about the robotics kits. The next semester, based on what she learned with and from her tech club members, Andrea is able to support use of the kits with all of her elementary students.

When Andrea described to us her own learning experience at the STEM institute, it was clear that it had been impactful. She left the institute wanting the learners in her classroom to feel the excitement that she felt in that moment—an excitement that she had not always felt in learning experiences, an excitement that propelled her to go home and continue to explore and create with the tools she had encountered. In thinking about the design of learning experiences, Andrea wants to create opportunities for the students in her classroom to feel excitement and a desire to learn more. Recognizing the parallel between what she wants for herself and what she wants for her students prompts Andrea to try out any new activity she might do with students before introducing it in her classroom. She does this so that she can understand what the process will feel like for her students, not just logistically, but also emotionally. When introducing new activities, Andrea prides herself in being able to share her own excitement with students, explaining that she is a learner alongside them and that there is nothing she will ask them to try that she hasn't tried herself.

In the moments with Andrea's students described in this vignette, we see how excitement enables learning and leads to learners' developing sense of competence and expertise. In the first instance, her student is so enthusiastic about his initial animation experiences that he invests more time, creating other projects and deepening his learning. It is important to him that Andrea is there to appreciate his creations, validating through her attention that his excitement is worth listening to, that it is pointing him in meaningful and productive directions. In the second instance, Andrea's response to her students' excitement about the robotics kits and their desire to share their knowledge with their classmates enables that excitement to have impacts not only for their own learning but for the class and school as well. Again, she validates the legitimacy of their excitement for robotics, inviting them to take ownership over structuring learning opportunities for others.

The importance of excitement in the classroom and the way in which making space for it facilitates learning was a central concern of renowned American cultural critic and feminist theorist bell hooks. hooks argued that for meaningful learning to occur, both teachers and students must have the space to be fully themselves in the classroom, in all the multidimensionality of their affective human experience. She asserted that powerful emotions—joy and excitement, anger and despair—both reflect and enable our engagement with the world, giving us information about what is important to us. But these feelings are not only information about or from individuals. In speaking of excitement specifically and its relationship to learning, hooks emphasized that excitement depends on every member of the classroom: "Excitement is generated through collective effort."[37]

According to hooks, this effort of cultivating excitement begins with recognition and acknowledgment. As she wrote in her 1994 essay collection *Teaching to Transgress*:

> As a classroom community, our capacity to generate excitement is deeply affected by our interest in one another, in hearing one another's voices, in recognizing one another's presence. Since the vast majority of students learn through conservative, traditional educational practices and concern themselves only with the presence of the professor, any radical pedagogy must insist that everyone's presence is acknowledged. That insistence cannot be simply stated. It has to be demonstrated through pedagogical practices. To begin, the professor must genuinely *value* everyone's presence. There must be an ongoing recognition that everyone influences the classroom dynamic, that everyone contributes. These contributions are resources. Used constructively they enhance the capacity of any class to create an open learning community.[38]

hooks further explained that recognition of the presence and contribution of every member of the learning community in this way necessitates a flexibility on the part of the teacher and the classroom: "Excitement could not be generated without a full recognition of the fact that there could never be an absolute set agenda governing teaching practices. Agendas had to be flexible, had to allow for spontaneous shifts in direction."[39] If we recognize the importance of excitement, then we need to be ready to pivot in moments when we don't encounter it or when we encounter it unexpectedly. We must be prepared to seek and follow excitement.

In Andrea's classroom, we see the power of this collective effort, and the reciprocity between the excitement the students bring and how her flexible responses to their excitement further fuel their sense of its importance for learning. Had the two students not seen the robotics kits and openly declared their enthusiasm for using them and helping others to do so, a learning opportunity would have been lost. When Andrea responds to them by saying, "Can you help us learn?" she is communicating to them how much she values them and what they can contribute to the learning community, and she enables their excitement to have real, material consequences for what she—and the entire learning community—does next. Rather than holding fast to her belief that she should experience new tools herself before trying them in the classroom, Andrea opens herself up to a new collaborative configuration for learning, inviting her two students to lead her and other students into exploration.

It is easy to trivialize excitement or to view it as incompatible with the work of the classroom. hooks acknowledged that excitement is seen "as potentially disruptive of the atmosphere of seriousness assumed to be essential to the learning process."[40] Although hooks was writing about her experiences of teaching college students, her call to make space for excitement, for learners' interests, passions, and enthusiasms, applies equally well and as urgently to K–12 classrooms. In the classroom as design studio, excitement is not in opposition to intellectual rigor, it is a necessary precondition. When teachers respond to students' expressions of excitement with the acknowledgment, validation, and encouragement that Andrea illustrated here, when they invite that excitement to impact the classroom and what happens in it, they communicate to learners that their excitement should be taken seriously, that it has much to tell them about what they can and should do.

WHAT CAN WE MAKE TOGETHER?

Torie, a high school software design teacher, has organized her year-long course as a mini start-up company, with the goal of launching an augmented reality app for the school community. At the beginning of the year, Torie interviews students to get a sense of them as individuals and where their particular interests, experiences, and strengths lie. She gives students a list of the possible jobs they can do as part of the larger project, including project managers, artists, graphic designers, implementation engineers, framework engineers, web administrators, and marketers. Based on the individual interviews and the preferences students indicate, Torie divides the students into teams that will be responsible for different aspects of the app, inviting them to think about a key question: "What can we make together?"

The project managers and marketing team members are less involved with coding but have the broadest perspective on the work of the group, understanding the functionality of the app being designed and imagining how it can be used by others The web administrators build and manage the team site that displays content related to the team projects, members, and mission. The artists and graphic designers understand the geometric capabilities of the augmented reality space and design original three-dimensional objects, film dances, and compose music to be incorporated into the application. The framework engineers write code for the specific features and functionalities designed by their classmates, and then pass their code to the implementation engineers to connect the code with content in the final application.

After assigning students to teams, the classroom is managed with a series of *sprints*, time-bounded periods to accomplish work. Each team is given a list of tasks to be completed by the end of a given sprint, working toward the launch of the app. Once the students have been given their tasks, Torie spends each class observing the groups, supporting students as needed, and helping teams think through how to prioritize tasks and do the work within a reasonable timeframe.

On a day in late March, the students are deep into their design work. Everyone knows their specific role in the development process and they come into the classroom, getting right into their respective tasks and activities. They move seamlessly between individual work and interaction with one another: checking in, consulting, coordinating, asking questions as they need to before moving back into their own piece of the project. Two students on the project management team sit in the back of the room, running through everything that has been done and needs to be done. They've built upon the team's work from the previous semester to create a color-coded system for organizing tasks: green is done, orange is waiting on another team so can't yet be done, yellow is in progress, red is not started. They are listing items and negotiating the colors to assign items on their chart, thinking through the big picture of what the class is doing and the specifics of each task.

In another part of the room, a student from the graphic design team is creating a 3D model of a building, having worked with his other team members earlier on to learn the design software he is using now. Nearby, two students finish their current tasks and go to join others at an adjacent table to see how they can help. The students they join express appreciation for their support and explain what they are currently working on. All four students sit quietly at the table working on their individual computers. In another area of the room where the implementation engineers have gathered, one student calls out to another that she's having difficulty with her code. Her colleague walks over, kneeling at the computer to read through the code and offer suggestions.

In Torie's classroom, students are engaged in a collective endeavor of creation while acting as individuals. Students are constantly making judgments and decisions about what they can and should do to advance the group project. Torie has intentionally designed the class to leave room for this kind of individuality, for students to be drawn to different elements of the work, and for those differences, collectively, to be a strength. When Torie told us about her motivation in designing the course, she mentioned feeling sure that there were students who "would have been great in a computer classroom, but they're not signing up for it." When she asked the students in her calculus class why so few of the girls had signed up for computer science electives relative to boys, many of them said, "I just don't think of myself as a tech person." The software development class is part of Torie's vision of inclusivity. She has a desire for more students to be able to see themselves in the work of computer science, contributing to software development through areas like artistic design and project management that students often don't think of as characterizing work in this field.

One of the most striking elements of this classroom is the self-directedness of the students. Torie isn't telling them what to do. When they have questions for her, she always tries to bring their questions to the group, underscoring the importance of their collective judgment about what should be done. The students are moving freely about the classroom, working on one thing and then another. They take time individually when the task demands it, as the student building the 3D model of a building has done. They similarly gather together when needed—when they need to learn (the design team using online tutorials to teach themselves a necessary tool), when they need to make collective decisions (the project management team working through items from their task management system), and when they feel in a position to offer support to others.

What would schooling be like if it were more centrally organized around the question "What can we make together?" In many respects, this is the question that American educational philosopher John Dewey explored in his 1900 text *The School and Society*, an early work describing the educational approach and practices of the University of Chicago Laboratory School that he helped establish. Dewey was motivated by two core concerns: how to make learning meaningful and connected to individuals and their daily lives, and how education could support the development and sustenance of a democratic society, one in which there was empathy and understanding across lines of difference and a sense of collective responsibility. He found that learning situations in which children were making things together as part of the collective, constructive activities of daily life (such as cooking, weaving, building) addressed both of these concerns. He described what it looked like when these activities were taking place, and the value that was possible:

There is little of one sort of order where things are in process of construction; there is a certain disorder to any busy workshop; there is not silence; persons are not engaged in maintaining certain fixed physical postures; their arms are not folded; they are not holding their books thus and so. They are doing a variety of things, and there is the confusion, the bustle, that results from activity. But out of the occupation, out of doing things that are to produce results, and out of doing these in a social and cooperative way, there is born a discipline of its own kind and type.[41]

There are multiple elements of Torie's classroom that reflect Dewey's description of this "busy workshop." Learners have a purpose that they have set for themselves, an end goal that is meaningful to them. In pursuit of this goal, they are engaged in a variety of activities, moving in and out of physical and social formations, working and talking as needed. But while acting independently, as individuals following their own judgment, learners are engaged in a collective endeavor. They care about what others are doing and what happens to them. They see the interdependence between their work and that of others.

Dewey contrasted this view of learning as meaningful collective construction with what he saw as the prevalence of learning experiences organized around individualized accumulation of knowledge with no discernable relevance to learners' lives and interests. Similarly, Torie described how the approach to learning in her software development class represented a cultural shift for her students. Most of their other educational experiences tended to be individualistic, experiences that she characterized as, "I have my task. It's the same as everybody else. I finished my worksheet. I'm done. I don't need to tell anybody about the fact that I'm done. It's done." In contrast, she wants them to experience in the software development project that what they do matters to what someone else is doing, because they are creating something together.

Torie noted that the course represented a shift in her own role as teacher as well. As she described:

My toughest role is at the beginning because I don't know who I'm going to get. Some of the kids I know. Some of them I don't. And then challenging myself, "How do I make this person feel valued?" I learn about their specific experiences and design a role that feels like they're authentically contributing to something.

What Torie emphasizes here is part of Dewey's reimagining of the role of the teacher in classrooms organized around meaningful collective construction. Core to Dewey's argument in *The School and Society* was a reclaiming of the intellectual nature of work that had been dismissed as "manual training,"[42] recognizing the ways that teachers were able to structure learning experiences that invited learners to engage with the work thoughtfully, on their own terms, rather than as fixed procedures and practices to be imitated. Torie is deeply concerned with her students as individuals, finding out who they are and how they can connect the work to their own interests and approaches. But these individual interests and inclinations are a place to start, not to end. In the design of this project, Torie is helping her students connect those interests to forms of thinking that may be new to them, enabling them to grow in their own capacity as learners and as software engineers, broadening their engagement with others and with the world.

WHAT DO YOU WANT TO BUILD TODAY?

Over the past several years, the students in Benjamin's STEM lab have been progressively building their understanding of coding and circuits. As second graders, they began coding using a visual programming language and they built physical circuits with breadboards and battery packs. Now, as third graders, they have started to integrate these two practices, programming simple computers to control LED lights powered by their circuits. In today's class, Benjamin's students are creating their own projects, guided by a prompt to make something that purposefully turns the LEDs on and off. Benjamin frames the task at the beginning of class with the invitation, "Today's your day to build and create. Take your time. Make it what you want it to be." He asks the students, "What do you want to build today?"

His students begin exploring, and they quickly become engrossed in trying to make their projects work. One pair of students spends most of the class period working to figure out how to get a red LED to turn on. One gestures to the screen as the other uses the mouse, talking together about what they are doing and how it is going. At one point, they swap control of the mouse, trying a few different directions, none of which work. They eventually swap again, and the student now controlling the mouse, inspired by the investigations, tries something new—and the light finally turns on. The students around them clap and cheer before turning their attention back to their work.

Elsewhere throughout the room, students are engaged in intense conversations with each other about elements of their projects, both aesthetic and computational. Two girls creating a scene that takes place in a bedroom animatedly debate about which sprites to use and why, with one student insisting on the specific placement of a bowl of cheese puffs on top of a dresser. A group creating a game based on a popular fantasy franchise discusses the ideal number of floating objects that should appear. A student from a group making a soccer quiz goes over to a group making a superhero quiz and learns how to link answering questions to turning the LEDs on.

As they work, Benjamin encourages his students to move around the room and interact with one another, inviting them to investigate what others are working on. Students see design features and elements that others have incorporated and want to learn how to do something similar in the context of their own project, asking excitedly, "Can I see it?" and "Oooh, how did you change the shape of that?"

In their work programming the LEDs, Benjamin encourages his students to pay attention to their own ideas and interests. As he explained, "I always emphasize that programming is a tool for the communication of ideas, thoughts, and feelings." The language Benjamin uses with his students as he frames the task reinforces this guiding principle, a reminder that they should be motivated by what they want to do and figure out, by what they want to build. He has set his students up for success both by building on their prior knowledge and experience and by offering them a prompt that matches their current skill level. In response, we see students able to take initiative in their problem-solving, excited by the technical possibilities they see around them and determined to figure out how to do new things and incorporate them into their own projects. The opportunity to craft their own designs at an appropriate challenge level invites Benjamin's students to work with focus and intensity, invested in the details of how their projects operate and look.

Being motivated by the pure enjoyment of creation and discovery is an important aspect of the human experience, as Hungarian-American psychologist and researcher of creativity Mihaly Csikszentmihalyi illuminated through his research. In the early 1990s, Csikszentmihalyi and his students at the University of Chicago conducted a multiyear, interview-based study of people renowned for their creativity. Although the participants of his study were, in his words, "exceptional individuals"[43] in terms of their creative reputations, many of the ideas from his work can help us understand creative work and process for everyone. Csikszentmihalyi's

1996 book based on the interviews, *Creativity: Flow and the Psychology of Discovery and Invention*, described the experience of *flow*, that is, being truly immersed in an activity that is an appropriate match to one's current skill level, not too easy and not too hard. It is an experience that Csikszentmihalyi argued was present in creative work across multiple domains—engineering and chemistry, writing and music, business and sociology, history and architecture. In a list of nine elements characteristic of the flow experience, Csikszentmihalyi identified the loss of self-consciousness one may experience:

> In everyday life, we are always monitoring how we appear to other people; we are on the alert to defend ourselves from potential slights and anxious to make a favorable impression. Typically this awareness of self is a burden. In flow we are too involved in what we are doing to care about protecting the ego. Yet after an episode of flow is over, we generally emerge from it with a stronger self-concept; we know that we have succeeded in meeting a difficult challenge.[44]

In Benjamin's classroom, we see this loss of self-consciousness. Benjamin's students aren't protecting their egos when they ask other students how to do something or compliment other students' creations. There is no evidence of students being worried about judgment from others or concerned about comparisons. They seem only interested in what they could learn that might help them figure out how to realize their own visions.

On this day in Benjamin's classroom, some students progress further along in their projects than others, and few finish. Some spend most of the period discussing a single aesthetic decision, and others leave their own work for a while to play a game their classmates have created and talk to them about it. Framed by Benjamin's reminders to "Take your time. Make it what you want it to be," the energy of the classroom isn't about accomplishment, it is about process, about the experience of creation, including confronting what one doesn't know and persevering in the challenges produced by that experience. While Csikszentmihalyi's research was conducted with people who were primarily defined by their accomplishments, by the external recognition of their creative work, Csikszentmihalyi surmised that we might all be happier if we related to our work and play without attention to those forms of external validation, if we allowed ourselves to feel the joy and satisfaction of learning and creation for its own sake. When we engage in an activity that produces the experience of flow, we want to do it more, because the experience itself is so enjoyable and meaningful. We see in Benjamin's classroom students experiencing the joy of creation—a joy that, as Csikszentmihalyi argued, will lead them to seek out further learning.

While Csikszentmihalyi expressed concern about the potential of traditional schooling to neglect, or even discourage, the experience of flow, he acknowledged the special role that a teacher can play in supporting young learners through noticing, care, and the environment that is established. Benjamin's classroom serves as an inspiring example of an environment that nurtures flow and creativity. We see in Benjamin's classroom an environment that enables learners to find what is beautiful about furthering one's own understanding through creation, including an embrace of the challenges that accompany the process.

We also see how Benjamin encourages interactions among his young creators. Although Csikszentmihalyi's research was focused on individuals and their creative processes, and his description of the experience of flow was primarily framed as an individual experience, he recognized the significance of access to and interactions with others.

> Yet over and over again, the importance of seeing people, hearing people, exchanging ideas, and getting to know another person's work and mind are stressed by creative individuals. The physicist John Wheeler expresses this point with his usual directness: "If you don't kick things around with people, you are out of it. Nobody, I always say, can be anybody without somebody being around."[45]

This is an essential quality of the classroom as design studio, exemplified by the classrooms of Benjamin and the other teachers we studied: the presence of others contributes to the excitement and the enjoyment of learning and creation. Benjamin described to us how students "can't resist bopping up to go tell somebody else what they figured out." In his classroom, others are an aid to an individual learner's processes of figuring things out—as resource, as inspiration, and as audience. And, remarkably, the presence of others does not diminish the loss of self-consciousness essential to being in flow. Learners in Benjamin's classroom do not lose their sense of what is important to them, of what they want to do, of themselves, in this community of creators.

WHY CAN'T A BOWL OF NOODLES BE A CHARACTER?

Throughout the year, Kara, a library media specialist, has noticed how engaged her fourth-grade students are when they have opportunities to express themselves and she has been thinking about how to support self-expression in coding activities, which they'll be starting soon as a group. She wants her students to enjoy their introduction to coding because she knows that as soon as they get turned off by something, it is incredibly hard to regain their interest and engagement. She decides to facilitate a coding project with her fourth graders that gives them broad guidelines for what to create: two characters encounter something unexpected and have a conversation about it. This project offers the students greater freedom than they have had before in both what they make and how they make it.

On the first day of the project, Kara is concerned that the students seem to be all over the place. They're adding ten characters instead of two. They're forgetting the unexpected element. Their characters are having conversations about anything other than what they've discovered. Some students are spending long periods of time on aesthetic elements, like coloring a character purple, and not working on programming the various elements of their projects. And by the end of class, many fewer students have completed the project than has happened during more structured assignments. When she stops by one student's computer, the student proudly displays their project, which features a bowl of noodles as one of the main characters. Kara groans inwardly, thinking to herself, "A bowl of noodles can't be a character." She worries that students' interests are distracting them from meaningful engagement with the underlying computational concepts.

After the students leave the room, Kara reflects on the session and her response to it. She wants to offer learners more freedom, but she is concerned about how they are using that freedom and its value to their learning. She thinks about the enthusiasm of her bowl-of-noodles student, a student who has rarely demonstrated passion and excitement in the classroom. She can imagine the impact of her skepticism—the light dimming in her student's eyes, their interest in pursuing the work further slipping away. She sits back in her chair and asks herself, "Well, why not? Why can't a bowl of noodles be a character?"

Although she is still nervous about whether students following their interests will result in meaningful learning of computational concepts and skills, Kara decides to continue with the project, maintaining her commitment to students' self-expression in the classroom. In their next session, the fourth graders bound into class. They're not only invested in the project and excited to keep working, but they also seem to know much more about the coding environment than they did before—how to insert characters, create text, and edit sprites. As she watches them work, she feels her worries and nervousness disappearing. Their open-ended explorations from the previous session have prepared them to focus on creating the scenes that will be their final projects and they are finding ways to express themselves with code that go far beyond what Kara had imagined. One student has characters stumble upon a pair of shoes, another has two mermaids find a seashell. One student codes a ten-minute play about a hedgehog and a penguin that go shopping on Black Friday and comment upon the absurdity of consumerism. A student who loves basketball spends thirty minutes coding an animation for an unexpected bouncing pattern his characters will discuss and is very proud of his creation.

Kara shared with us that she knew she wanted to make greater space in her teaching for learners' self-expression, for their interests and their ideas. In response, she tried something new, with a project in which students exercise much greater choice and discretion in what they make and how they make it. But she wrestled with the extent to which this change in her practice created greater uncertainty in the classroom. She considered the students' response to the new opportunity along multiple dimensions—the greater chaos in the classroom and less linear progression on the assignment but also the greater joy and enthusiasm and personally meaningful engagement with computational concepts.

With her new approach, Kara had to grapple with the meaning that students' work held for them, and the ways that meaning might be different from her own. Kara was thinking about her students' experiences, but also her own ideas and understandings of the relationship between creative expression and computer science, about what counts as legitimate and meaningful learning. For her students, spending time on the color of a sprite was central to realizing their creative vision, and creating a story about a bowl of noodles as a main character was their way of engaging with the coding project. At first, Kara didn't see these choices as valuable to learning, but through a process of careful noticing, reflecting, and experimenting, she came to recognize and appreciate the value these choices held for her students.

Donald Schön was an American philosopher whose work contributed to understandings of the complexity and uncertainty inherent in professional practice, such as teaching. His writing helps us understand that complexity and uncertainty are not things to be avoided; instead, by recognizing complexity and uncertainty in our work, we are better prepared to respond to such circumstances in meaningful and productive ways, by acting as *reflective practitioners*.[46] The reflective practitioner is one who acts as an inquirer, engaging in careful noticing, allowing those observations to change their own thinking and action. In his 1983 book *The Reflective Practitioner: How Professionals Think in Action*, Schön described the key work of the reflective practitioner—that is, reflection-in-action—as follows:

> Both ordinary people and professional practitioners often think about what they are doing, sometimes even while doing it. Stimulated by surprise, they turn thought back on action and on the knowing which is implicit in action. They may ask themselves, for example, "What features do I notice when I recognize this thing? What are the criteria by which I make this judgment? What procedures am I enacting when I perform this skill? How am I framing the problem that I am trying to solve?" Usually reflection on knowing-in-action goes together with reflection on the stuff at hand. There is some puzzling, or troubling, or interesting phenomenon with which the individual is trying to deal. As he tries to make sense of it, he also reflects on the understandings which have been implicit in his action, understandings which he surfaces, criticizes, restructures, and embodies in further action. It is this entire process of reflection-in-action which is central to the "art" by which practitioners sometimes deal well with situations of uncertainty, instability, uniqueness, and value conflict.[47]

Schön contrasted this model of reflective practice with a model of *technical rationality* in which practitioners see their work as applying a previously developed set of actions or approaches to a given situation to produce predetermined outcomes. But teaching is not the act of applying a formula or an algorithm to a situation; it is more experimental, improvisational, drawing on professional expertise in response to a situation. "In the most generic sense," Schön wrote, "to experiment is to act in order to see what the action leads to. The most fundamental experimental question is, 'What if?'"[48] We see this experimental stance at work in the learning experience Kara has designed for her fourth graders. Taking seriously the ideas of her students about what they want to create and how prompts Kara to further reflect on the multiple considerations of her own practice—questioning, wondering, and being open to new ways of doing things.

Perhaps most significantly, engaging in this process of reflective practice leads Kara to new ways of thinking about learning, especially the relationship between creative expression and computational understanding. As Schön observed, reflection can prompt a destabilization of how practitioners think about what we think we know, including even the most fundamental goals and values of our practice and field. This can be unsettling but also, as we see in Kara's classroom, ultimately rewarding. Kara had noticed how much happier and more engaged learners were doing projects that involved more self-direction and self-expression and felt that, without those elements, it was harder for other learning to occur. She had initially worried about what she saw as a potential conflict between the excitement that students demonstrated when following their interests and their learning of necessary computational concepts and skills. But as she allowed the project to play out, thereby engaging in her own "What if?" experiment, she came to see how their personal interests could, in fact, be supportive of their computational learning. As she described, "The fact that I let them go crazy creatively made them more effective and interested in coding and computer science. I think now that creativity is not only a powerful thing on its own, but it can actually enhance the skills and experience that students interact with."

WHAT DID YOU TRY?

For several class sessions, Allison's seventh graders have been working with partners to create projects of their choice using a simulation programming environment. At the beginning of today's class, Allison invites her students to the front of the room for a quick whole-group check-in, knowing that learners are in very different places in terms of their project development and comfort with coding. She reminds students about the upcoming presentation of their programs and polls students to see how they are feeling about their progress.

After the whole-group conversation, students make their way to their computers with their partners. Allison heads over to one pair who had shared that they were struggling with creating a simulation of gravity that they felt was sufficiently realistic. When she sits down with them, the students run their program for Allison. She invites them to read their code out loud and, as they read, she occasionally pauses them to ask questions about their modeling decisions and to discuss why the agents in their project don't look real. She asks them to think about how gravity affects their bodies. When the students look uncertain, Allison stands up from her chair and asks whether gravity is affecting her. She then stands on a chair and jumps down, prompting the students to consider the difference between her actions and the agents in their program. The students' eyes light up with inspiration. They start making changes to their code and Allison leaves to check in with other students.

Allison eventually makes her way back to the two students working on their gravity modeling. "Okay—what did you try?" she asks. They have made progress with their project, but her students are still struggling with making gravity look as realistic as they would like. Allison goes back to her desk and emails several example projects to the duo. When she returns to them, her students are already trying out the projects she sent. "Don't just click everything," she reminds them. "Look at the code and try to figure it out." As she listens to their discussion of the code, Allison has another idea for how to support them. "Oh! I think I know what you're looking for," she says. She grabs a stack of the help cards from the front table and flips to a specific card. "Play around with this," she says. "It's not exactly the same but I think it'll help."

In the classroom as design studio, students are often, and perhaps even ideally, operating at the leading edge of their current understanding and capability as they work to bring their ideas into the world through their creations. What is so important about this kind of learning environment is that the conception of what students are capable of need not be limited to the individual students; students are supported by other people and their capabilities are, as a result, extended and expanded. Lev Vygotsky, the early twentieth-century Russian developmental psychologist, offered us a name for this way of conceptualizing present and possible capability through supportive others: the *zone of proximal development*. In *Mind in Society*, a translated collection of Vygotsky's essays published more than forty years after his death, Vygotsky defined the zone of proximal development (popularly referred to as ZPD) as "the distance between the actual developmental level as determined by independent problem solving and the level of potential development as determined through problem solving under adult guidance or in collaboration with more capable peers."[49] With his work, Vygotsky was responding to the prevailing conceptions of his era, which viewed learner capability (and, in turn, measures of that capability) as primarily individual. If we really want to understand what learners are capable of, his argument went, we must think not only of what learners are able to accomplish independently, but also what they can achieve in concert with guidance from others.

Our view into Allison's classroom shows us what adult guidance can look like. It begins with Allison's assessment of her students' current progress. We see this in her opening class meeting, which then leads to her interactions with the partners working on their gravity problem. Both in the whole group and in this more focused interaction with the gravity pair, Allison begins by asking questions and listening to understand where her students are and what they might need. From there, we see Allison utilize a wide variety of strategies to help the partners make progress: inviting students to read their code aloud, engaging in physical modeling, asking reflective questions, giving time for exploration, sharing sample projects, and offering resource materials. She draws on these different interventions in response to what she is seeing in her students, her sense of what they need, and then adjusting when a support isn't able to help them go further. This isn't doing the work for them, undermining their sense of capability and possibility. Instead, she's offering help and resources so they can expand what they are capable of, working in the service of their own vision for their project.

Allison's dynamic and responsive guidance is enabled by her knowledge and experience as a teacher. But it is also enabled by the culture she has created within the classroom, one in which, as Vygotsky affirmed, peers are an additional important resource for supporting learners. In our conversations with Allison, she described the intentionality with which she attended to student experience and expertise, inviting students to share what they know with others in their classroom community, including herself.

> When I notice students who are experts at a particular thing, I ask them to share their knowledge with the class or particular other students who would like to learn what that student just learned. I have had students teach me things that I haven't had time to explore. For example, if a student asks me if a tool can do a certain thing, I tell them what I know about it and have them investigate to make it work. When it works, I ask that student to share that knowledge with other interested students and me. When I share it with the other classes, I always give credit to the student and let the student know my other classes also appreciate what they learned. It is very exciting for all of us in class to learn that way and I have learned how to do many things that I just don't have time to sit down and figure out.

Describing how students in her classroom had internalized this culture, Allison told us about a student who, during this unit, showed her a project he had made at home that used gravity in a very different way than was described on the reference cards. He told her, "I made this because I noticed kids were struggling," and was excited to share the project with others. This sense of collective responsibility influences how Allison can think about her own deployment of time and attention in the classroom. On the day described in the vignette, she spent a significant amount of time with two students on their project, trying to get a sense of their understanding and figuring out ways to help them move forward. She was able to do this because she was not the only resource available, thanks to the strong peer-learning culture. She also knew that this time was a potential investment—on another day, those two students might then be able to help others, freeing her time and attention for other students and other needs.

Vygotsky's contributions to learning theory help us appreciate that the fullest expression of what we are capable of comes not when we are alone, but when we are with others. And he offered the concept of the zone of proximal development as part of an argument about what is so special about school, about how school can contribute to development in wonderful ways. So many of the qualities we emphasize in our descriptions of the classroom as design studio—freedom, choice, interest, expression—are often associated with out-of-school learning experiences. What we see in Allison's classroom is not only that such qualities are possible within school environments, but rather that the qualities can be particularly, essentially, enabled by school itself. Allison is listening to her students, responding to what they say they want to do and what they are actually doing. She is attending to, as Vygotsky phrased it, "how developmental processes stimulated by the course of school learning are carried through inside the head of each individual child."[50] In so doing, she is supporting them in reaching beyond the limits of their present understanding in ways that were made possible through the culture of collective problem-solving that she has fostered in her classroom community.

DID YOU MAKE THE MUSIC COME OUT LIKE YOU WANTED?

As her middle school's technology teacher, Tamara has spent the last several years getting to know her eighth graders through the work they are doing in class. When they first learn to use email, she asks them to write letters to their future graduating eighth-grade selves. When they begin designing presentations with digital slide decks, she structures the first project as a journal about their daily lives. She invites them to use a drawing program to create characters that they can then use in other animations, encouraging them to find inspiration in whatever brings them joy. And, throughout each day, Tamara talks to her students about their lives, learning about what draws their time and attention in and out of school—like sports or music—and asking them about significant events, like one student's recent admissions interview at a STEM high school.

The eighth-grade students in Tamara's technology class are starting a new media design project, choosing both the topic of their project and the digital tool they will use. "Think of something that you love," Tamara encourages her eighth graders as they start imagining the possibilities. A few weeks into the design project, students have focused on their topics of interest, topics that matter to them. One student is creating an interactive softball simulation, experimenting with modeling her experiences with the sport. Another student is working on a game inspired by his favorite sci-fi film series. One student, a musician, is hand-drawing a cello, instead of using preexisting images available in the graphics library, and coding a melodic line, instead of using prerecorded audio.

Toward the end of the session, Tamara encourages her students to save their work and get ready for their next class. "Turn to someone and tell them one thing you learned today," Tamara suggests. Students reluctantly pull themselves away from their projects, packing up their notebooks and peering over at others' computers to share what progress has been made. As Tamara listens across their conversations, she hears students who are often reluctant to speak chatting enthusiastically about their projects. As her eighth graders file out of the room and her sixth graders bustle in, Tamara calls out to the student who has been working on the cello, asking, "Did you make the music come out like you wanted?" "Not yet," he says, but he clearly sounds excited to keep trying.

The work of the classroom as design studio begins with each individual learner—what questions they have, what they're curious about, what matters to them. In the way she structures and frames the media design and other projects, Tamara is asking her students who they are and what they care about, communicating that their answers to those questions matter to her, and that they should and will guide the work in their classroom. Asking the student, "Did you make the music come out like you wanted?" conveys her attention to this individual and his project, her awareness of what is meaningful and important to him, and her support for his focusing on those things in his work. Tamara's conviction about the importance of learners connecting themselves as people to their work in the classroom is grounded in her understanding of the particular needs of middle schoolers, an age group that she especially loves. It isn't only that students are more invested in learning when it feels connected to them; middle school is an important time of self-discovery and identity work for students. As Tamara explained to us, "This is when they find out who they are as students and people before high school." Many students engage in this identity work through projects that are connected to their interests—the activities and emblems of popular culture that are part of how they see themselves and present themselves to others. But the space that Tamara creates in these projects also enables more expansive explorations of what matters to learners. For instance, a student who initially began making a project about an activity he enjoyed (soccer) decided instead to use the project as an opportunity to think through his upcoming individualized education program (IEP) meeting, where he would be sharing his goals for and progress in his learning.

In Tamara's classroom, the projects that students make, and what they choose to code, to animate, to create, are a form of self-expression. The projects are a way for students to find and use their voice, to show who they are, both to themselves and to others. But she also sees the risks that can accompany self-expression, as the insecurities and uncertainties raised by this identity work may overwhelm learners' own interests, nudging them toward conforming behavior that, while potentially cultivating a greater sense of self-protection and security, may be less aligned with what they care about. Part of what made Tamara proud of her eighth graders in this project was that they allowed themselves to explore what they actually cared about, as illustrated by the student who made the project about his IEP goals, and to not be deterred or distracted by what others were doing or the visibility that came with sharing a part of themselves. As Tamara noted, "When I look around the room, they're all doing something different. That makes me actually so happy. Because often, nobody wants to be seen, like, 'Don't look at me. I don't want to stand out in middle school.'"

In her 1977 paper *The Transformation of Silence into Language and Action*, the self-described "Black, lesbian, feminist, socialist, poet, mother"[51] Audre Lorde helps us understand the relationship between the barriers to expressing ourselves and the urgent necessity of doing so. Bringing our ideas into the world makes us vulnerable to others; we share something of ourselves, which can feel dangerous. But the alternative is fundamentally at odds with honoring one's self. As Lorde shared with her audience:

> And of course I am afraid, because the transformation of silence into language and action is an act of self-revelation, and that always seems fraught with danger. But my daughter, when I told her of our topic and my difficulty with it, said, "Tell them about how you're never really a whole person if you remain silent, because there's always that one little piece inside you that wants to be spoken out."[52]

By encouraging her students to surface and pursue their cares and concerns through their creations, Tamara is honoring her students as whole people. She creates a learning environment where they can figure out what they need to say and then are supported in the work of saying it.

The costs of not speaking, the costs of hiding in fear from the visibility that expressing ourselves brings, are levied not only on us, but also on our connections with others. As Lorde wrote, "It is not difference which immobilizes us, but silence."[53] Tamara spoke about the worry her students have that someone else will judge them for expressing themselves. But we also see in her classroom how working on something they care about helps students come alive and connect with one another, as they engage with interest in the work that their peers are doing. Students want to show each other what they are working on, including those who can sometimes be reluctant to speak up. Students are interested in their classmates' projects, eager to turn to someone else and learn about what they are doing. Students' self-expression also forms the basis of the connection between the students and Tamara herself. All the moves that we see Tamara make here—the open-ended design of the eighth-grade projects, the framing of the work as being about finding what you love, asking students about their lives, following up with them about what they have done in and out of class—are ways to know them, to know who they are, to support them in expressing a self in the classroom.

The classroom as design studio is a space where learners can be who they are, and express the things that are important to them. As teachers, we invite and validate that expression through the projects and learning opportunities we create for students, and how we interact with our students. In our conversations with her, Tamara connected her organization of projects around self-expression to how she interacted with students whose behavior might be considered difficult or disruptive in traditional learning spaces—loud voices and active bodies, expressions of intense emotion. She explained:

> I think the way you treat the kids that are maybe having a hard time sets a tone. And if they feel comfortable to express themselves and be themselves, I think that has to do with if your students are going to show you their real voice or not.

Tamara's description of how she creates a different culture of learning than students sometimes have access to—one in which who they actually are, what they are actually feeling, what they actually care about is of the utmost importance to their teacher and to the learning process—gestures to the painful alternative for educational environments to punish the expression of self through rigid control of students' bodies and voices, of students' thinking, speaking, doing, and being. Instead, as teachers, we can create classrooms that are spaces of self-expression, building the kind of trust with our students that enables them to speak their true voices, to show us who they really are. It is through that trust that they can, in Lorde's words, embrace language and action over silence.

THAT LOOKS AWESOME! WHAT WILL HAPPEN NEXT?

Elementary technology teacher Melanie offers the learners in her classroom choices for what they create through projects that students can take in many different directions, such as designing animations to accompany an inspirational song or creating their own robotic dolls. At the beginning of the year, students often respond to this open-endedness with hesitancy and even reluctance, unsure of what it means to follow their ideas and fearful of doing something that isn't what they think they are being asked to do. Melanie responds with steady encouragement and validation. "You're doing great in this," she tells them. As the year progresses, students develop greater comfort and confidence with uncertainty. They are increasingly able to dive in without fear, figuring things out as they need to, and enjoying the opportunity to explore.

On a morning in mid-February, Melanie's fifth graders are busy coding animations that demonstrate elements of the food chain. As she wanders around the room, Melanie admires the wide range of topics and approaches her students are exploring. She watches and listens, appreciating what she is seeing and offering questions to help students move forward.

Melanie asks one pair of students what they're working on. "We took almost a whole class period just to draw the snail!," one of the students exclaims. Melanie nods reassuringly as she appraises the snail on screen, "I love it. Maybe we'll showcase it at the end of class?" Another pair shouts out, "We're done!" Melanie excitedly moves over to where they are working and tries their game. She asks them several questions about their design decisions. Afterward, she says, "I love how you explained all of your choices! That rocked! Do you have anything else you want to add to the project?" Finally, she wanders over to another pair, two girls working on a project about the tapir. They show Melanie the animation they've developed so far. Melanie smiles and says, "That looks awesome! What will happen next?"

The open-endedness of the projects into which Melanie invites her students purposefully creates space for them to take things in their own direction, to figure out what the project means and looks like to them. This kind of freedom can be destabilizing as well as exhilarating, as learners have to rely on their own judgment and discretion rather than external validation that they are doing what is expected. In our conversations with her, Melanie explained that the kind of affirmation she offered students here is intended to enable them to deal with the uncertainty endemic to learning in the classroom as design studio. Her affirmations are a direct response to the worry that she sees in them, a way of encouraging her students to let go of being concerned with getting things either right or wrong. She shared with us that "by saying to them, 'This is great,' it's making them okay. Even when they make mistakes—it's great, let's fix it."

Melanie has found that this validation is especially necessary at the beginning of the year, when students need support and encouragement to even be able to try. As the year progresses, Melanie maintains a culture of affirmation, but she shifts her mode of interaction with the students slightly. She engages with the specifics of their projects, again encouraging and affirming, helping them feel good about what they've been able to accomplish, but also helping them look forward, asking questions that prompt them to think about what they might do next. Some students may not have been ready for these kinds of prompting questions earlier in the year, needing to feel more secure in their abilities to engage in this kind of work. But, now that they are more confident, Melanie continues to affirm what they've done while also prompting them to think about how they could improve.

While Melanie underscored the importance of affirmations, these affirmations would not have had meaning without the deep attention behind them. It isn't just that Melanie is telling learners their projects are awesome or that a piece of work is great or that she loves something she's looking at; these affirmations come after she has spent time with them, looking at what they've done and listening to them talk about it, really taking in the work and their relationship to it. That attention is, in itself, affirming, separate from the words that may follow it. In his book *Pedagogy of Freedom*, published in 1998 shortly after his death, Brazilian teacher and educational theorist Paulo Freire highlighted the importance of this attention to the work of teaching, and its attendant impact on learners' sense of themselves and belief in their own capacity. Relating a story from his own adolescence, Freire shared:

> Sometimes a simple, almost insignificant gesture on the part of a teacher can have a profound formative effect on the life of a student. I will always remember one such gesture in my life when I was an adolescent. A gesture that marks me profoundly but whose significance on my life was almost certainly not noticed or known by my teacher. At that time I experienced myself as an insecure adolescent, not at home with a body perceived as more bone than beauty, feeling myself to be less capable than the other students, insecure about my own creative possibilities, easily riled, and not very much at peace with the world. . . . On this occasion our teacher had brought our homework to school after correcting it and was calling us one by one to comment on it. When my turn came, I noticed he was looking over my text with great attention, nodding his head in an attitude of respect and consideration. His respectful and appreciative attitude had a much greater effect on me than the high classification that he gave me for my work. The gesture of the teacher affirmed in me a self-confidence that obviously still had much room to grow. But it inspired in me a belief that I too had value and could work and produce results—results that clearly had their limits but that were a demonstration of my capacity, which up until that moment I would have been inclined to hide or not fully believe in. And the greatest proof of the importance of that gesture is that I can speak of it now as if it had happened only today.[54]

As Freire noted, it was the teacher's focus on him, the attitude of "respect and consideration" for him and his work, that made an even deeper impact on his belief in himself than the grade on his work. This is what we see Melanie doing in her classroom: paying careful, focused attention to learners and their work, and offering words that recognize and affirm what learners have done. She is communicating to them her trust that they are capable, even if what they are making is still a work in progress. She is inspiring confidence and helping them let go of their worries about making mistakes, about doing things "wrong."

As Freire articulated, the importance of his teacher's affirmation wasn't about the specific piece of work that the teacher responded to—the power of the affirmation was the confidence it inspired to move forward with future learning. The work of affirmation in the classroom as design studio is about this forward orientation, about helping learners feel secure, not in a way that promotes complacency, but with confidence that they can and should attempt the unknown, that something meaningful and valuable will occur in the endeavor, even if they don't yet know exactly what it is. This type of affirmation, as advocated by Freire and as seen in Melanie's classroom, avoids a potential pitfall of praise in classrooms, where affirmation can be used (intentionally or not) to coerce or control, to direct students to do one thing rather than another. What is so remarkable in the way that Melanie converses with her students about their projects is her coupling of affirmation with looking forward, her assertion "That looks awesome!" followed by the question "What will happen next?" This question is genuinely open-ended. She doesn't know what they will do next, and her aim is to affirm their belief in their own capacity to figure it out for themselves. Her words reflect the seriousness with which she is taking the learners and their work—a wondering about future possibilities inspired by the interesting ideas contained within the students' own creations. Through these forward-looking questions, Melanie is fostering in her students the curiosity that is central to the educational endeavor. As Freire described it:

> Curiosity as restless questioning, as movement toward the revelation of something hidden, as a question verbalized or not, as search for clarity, as a moment of attention, suggestion, and vigilance, constitutes an integral part of the phenomenon of being alive. There could be no creativity without the curiosity that moves us and sets us patiently impatient before a world that we did not make, to add to it something of our own making.[55]

It is this curiosity, this interest in what might be, that is the antidote to the preoccupation with being right and fear of being wrong that Melanie observes as so limiting and so stressful and so unsatisfying for her students. As Freire emphasized, it is this curiosity about what we don't know and haven't done that prompts us to want to create and make, to engage with the world.

Paulo Freire is deeply identified with learner-centered teaching, with taking learners and their ideas seriously. But another theme throughout Freire's work is caution against educators thinking that to center learners' ideas and selves in the classroom, to believe in the teacher as fellow learner, means to deny the real, material difference between teacher and student, a difference of position, of power, a difference of responsibility. As teachers in learner-centered classrooms, we are sometimes uncomfortable with the idea of these differences. We want to shy away from them because we see how they have been used to limit, to shut down, learners' self-determination and self-expression, and that is exactly what we don't want to do. But to deny one's own power as a teacher is to deny one's students the opportunity for the necessary affirmation that Melanie offers here. This is the beauty of what we get to do with our power—we get to help learners believe in themselves.

WHAT'S UP?

Students in Nathan's high school computer science class have been working on learning to program using a text-based coding environment. One student, new to the school, has been a reluctant participant from the beginning and, over the past week, has stopped turning in any work. Nathan recognizes that this student is shy and has been somewhat disconnected from the classroom community, opting to work alone rather than with a partner. He worries that she won't initiate a conversation with him about what is happening and how things are for her.

He approaches her during class, while other students are engaged in their work, and gently asks without judgment, "What's up?" The student explains that she really wants to learn computer programming but doesn't like the work they're doing with this language. Nathan nods and makes a series of suggestions about other ways to move forward with the present curriculum, but she quietly rejects each suggestion. Recognizing that sticking with the current curriculum and the text-based environment isn't going to work for this student, Nathan introduces the student to a visual programming language as an alternative, which she seems cautiously curious about. He provides her with a small set of introductory assignments to help her learn the basics of the language and then encourages her to make what she wants with it.

The student responds to the new programming environment with interest and motivation that had been entirely absent before, remarking, "I can do some things I really want here." Being able to express herself with this alternative tool enables the student to build projects of increasing complexity over the course of the semester. In one of her final projects, she uses the drawing feature of the program to draw many frames of a fox running and posing, which she assembles into an animation, complete with coordinated music. With this new interest in computer science, she goes on to take Nathan's web design class the following semester.

Nathan wanted this student, like all his students, to emerge from his class with a deepened understanding of programming. But he recognized that she could not begin to develop that understanding until she was able to find a computational medium in which she could start creating the projects that she cared about, in which she could express herself. And she wasn't able to find that medium on her own.

Friedrich Froebel, pioneering early childhood educator and inventor of kindergarten, believed that one of the fundamental impulses of children is the drive to express what is inside them, to manifest their selves in the material world around them. In a posthumous collection of his writing, Froebel offered that:

> The genuinely healthy child will be always active, he will employ himself. Why? He wishes to make something so that his inward desire may appear externally. He wishes that what is hidden within him, and lives in him, may also outwardly exist.[56]

Froebel argued that learning opportunities should be responsive to these innate impulses of the child by encouraging play, exploration, and creation. This conception of children and its implications for education were notably different from the teacher-directed rote instruction observed by Froebel in German educational experiences of the late eighteenth century and early nineteenth century.

Across a set of core texts—*Education of Man, Pedagogics of the Kindergarten,* and *Education by Development*—Froebel explored the pedagogical implications of this understanding of young people, this respect for what is inside of them. He acknowledged the complexity and even seeming contradiction of what it means to support learners in being self-directed, especially when they might not yet have the capacity to achieve what they want to. The work of the adult, then, is to notice what young learners need and—though their ideas may not yet be fully formed—to help give them language to express both their ambitions and the challenges to realizing those ambitions.

This vignette highlights the multiple aspects of Nathan's response that supported his student in finding a way into programming that worked for her, enabling her to see herself in the work. First, Nathan notices that something isn't working for her. He then approaches her directly and engages with her in a way that is open and invites a genuine answer to his question about what she is experiencing. He listens to her, taking seriously what she is saying about her own aspirations for computer science and the fact that the text-based coding language and curriculum simply aren't working for her, and, in her assessment, won't work for her. And finally, he suggests an alternative path, helping the student connect to a medium where she can express herself and feel connected to her broader interest in the field.

When Nathan approached this student, when he asked her what was going on, he didn't know the answer. He didn't know what exactly it was that the student wanted to express and hadn't been able to, because she herself couldn't express it yet. Our support of young people in becoming who they are happens absent a certainty of exactly who that self is, of who they will become. That our work as educators is in the service of development of which we cannot see the end is reflected in a core metaphor that Froebel used throughout his work, of the child as seed kernel:

> But we cultivate a *kernel*, a *grain* of *corn*, just on account of its *innermost*, of its *life*; though that life exists in it as yet so enveloped and, as it were, so veiled; though the form of life hidden within it be invisible and unrecognizable. We cultivate it that it may unfold before us its life, its nature, in forms, unhindered, with force and spontaneous action, as truly as perceptibly and as beautifully as powerfully. We remove everything from it which might disturb and stifle, or even only unnaturally check, this free, spontaneous, independent development in harmony with the whole; and all this we do so much the more when the kernel, or corn, is the seed of a plant as yet unknown to us in its whole nature.[57]

As Froebel emphasized, the way to support someone on their journey toward a destination we cannot see is to take seriously the impulses of development coming from the young person themselves, to respond to what they are drawn to, to their expressions even in their most nascent and emerging forms. And we can't do that without really, truly, listening to them, as Nathan does here with this student. It was not only that listening helped Nathan figure out an alternative coding environment that might work better for the student, but also that his listening cultivated her interests and impulses, in a way that enabled her to maintain a connection to programming and computer science.

Learners need our support, our careful attention, to find themselves in the work, to figure out how to connect who they are and what they want with the broader ideas about which they are learning. Trust in their potential growth—even when at first "invisible and unrecognizable"[58]—lies at the heart of the classroom as design studio.

WHAT HAVE OTHERS DONE?

The high school students in Alan's AP Computer Science A class are learning the concept of recursion. To support their learning, Alan prepares an assignment in which students create trees using fractals, designs that repeat on a continually decreasing scale. Alan describes the basic design of a fractal tree, where a vertical line branches off into two smaller lines at the top, with each branching off into two smaller lines, and so on. But he encourages the students to customize their fractal trees, using code to experiment with branch length and width, the angle that separates the two branches, while also adding an additional branch, or introducing randomness to the fractal process. "Your fractal tree doesn't have to look like any other," he tells them.

As with all of Alan's assignments, the web page that describes the assignment links to an online repository of more than a hundred examples of past students' work. He invites them to begin by exploring. "Take a look. What have others done?" Students begin by looking through the many online examples, finding ideas that inspire them and approaches they may not have imagined.

After several class periods, the assignment nears its end and Alan calls the class's attention back to the online repository of student work, where he has now linked their fractal trees. The fractal trees the students have created are beautiful, each incredibly unique. One student decided to add a third branch at each junction of her dark red tree, creating a brush-like effect at the top. A second student used randomness to subtly change the branching angle, resulting in a surprisingly realistic black-and-white tree. Another student used randomness and decreasing branch thickness, creating an otherworldly tree with sparse green branches that looked like it was lit from underneath. A fourth student didn't use any straight lines in his tree, with every branch, large and small, curving in different ways.

After highlighting these examples, Alan says to his students, "I've shown you a few examples, but I really encourage you to go back to the page and look at what students in this classroom have done, because it's really cool. You all have done really neat stuff that I wouldn't have anticipated or expected, so you should take some class time to take a look at that." Even though the assignment is technically over, students continue to return to their fractal trees and revise what they've done, inspired by others' work and wanting to improve their contribution to the online collection.

As a teacher of AP Computer Science A, Alan is necessarily focused on supporting students in learning, understanding, and utilizing specific computer science concepts. But that conceptual focus is not in conflict with a desire to honor students' creative aims and individual styles. As reflected in the diversity of his students' fractal trees, they were still able to develop projects that represented their own unique approaches. When we asked Alan what enabled this kind of creative expression and personalization, he attributed it to his use of the online repository and to his encouragement of students to examine others' work. Alan observed:

> The thing that's most successful for me is for students to see other students' work. I think creativity doesn't necessarily work best in a vacuum. I think it's good to be in a space where other people are doing things as well. There's excitement in working on something when other people are working on it, and working together, but also being different and doing your own thing. So I think the thing that works best for me is just that opportunity for students to see each other's work and talk about it, and share and build.

As Alan articulates here, engaging with others' work has impacts along multiple dimensions. It can serve as inspiration, expanding students' sense of creative possibilities. It can fuel excitement and motivation, through the students' sense of shared endeavor and an awareness of the value their work holds for others.

An ostensible contradiction of the classroom as design studio is that encountering the ideas and practices of others is an important catalyst for learners to develop their own ideas and practices. Alan understands this interdependence and has designed his classroom around it. He encourages students to find themselves in their projects. He assigns individual work, prompting students to work independently. But simultaneously, by working around others and engaging with their work, Alan's students are working in connection rather than isolation—a connection that enables the interchange of ideas, excitement, appreciation, and affective support.

It is this kind of interconnection among learners—an expanded conception of who we can learn from and when in the service of our goals as learners—that Austrian philosopher and theologian Ivan Illich described in his 1970 book *Deschooling Society*. In making his radical call for an end to compulsory, institutionalized schooling, Illich was fundamentally concerned with the way such institutionalization created scarcity around both learning and teaching, making people think that there were only certain times and circumstances under which they could learn from certain designated people. Asserting unequivocally that "education for all means education by all,"[59] Illich imagined alternative structures that served his understanding of the purpose of the educational system, that "it should provide all who want to learn with access to available resources at any time in their lives" and "empower all who want to share what they know to find those who want to learn it from them."[60] In response to the institutionalization he observed, he offered a vision of a very different social organization of learning, which he called *learning webs*, networks that connected people to the materials, peers, and teachers they needed to help them learn what and when they wanted. As he described:

> The current search for new educational funnels must be reversed into the search for their institutional inverse: educational webs which heighten the opportunity for each one to transform each moment of his living into one of learning, sharing, and caring.[61]

In these learning webs, Illich imagined learners as "independent, yet related to each other."[62] This is an elegant and succinct articulation of the relationships between learners in classrooms such as Alan's, where learners are developing their own ideas and selves, while simultaneously developing awareness of how the people around them might contribute to that process.

Illich was prescient about how technology could support the autonomously navigated connections embodied in these learning webs. For example, Illich envisioned computer-supported networks through which learners could access models of the work they wanted to do, and connect with peers to engage in that work alongside them. Part of what is notable in Alan's use of the online repository—a professional tool, not specifically designed for use by students—is the sheer number of examples of student work he is able to maintain. He doesn't limit or curate the examples. Alan sees the volume and range of examples as especially enabling of students' creative imaginations, supporting the development of their individual visions for the work. This way of using examples invites learners themselves to figure out what they need for their own learning, to make choices about what is and is not interesting and valuable to them.

Alan acknowledged that his approach depends on trusting learners to take what they need from the examples of others, including looking at the code their peers have used to create a specific design; it is a trust that learners will use examples to advance their own learning, rather than as a shortcut or a way to avoid figuring things out for themselves. He understood the questions and worries within the computer science community about when and how it is appropriate for students to look at and use one another's code. But, he explained, such worries seemed to be less relevant when the whole purpose of the project was for students to create something of their own and present it to others.

Illich argued that the problems of motivation reported by many traditional educational institutions (he spoke especially about high rates of young people dropping out of school) were problems of schooling, not of learning. That is, what was causing people to not engage with school, or engage with it in an oppositional or unsatisfying manner, was not learning itself but the ways in which their opportunities to learn were designed and structured. Illich believed that people are intrinsically motivated both to learn how to do things they are interested in, that are meaningful to them for their own purposes, and to support the learning of others, to share what they know.

This is another way in which the purpose of learning in the classroom as design studio—to figure out what you want, what you need, what you care about—invites learners into different kinds of relationships to learning and with one another: relationships in which the examples of others enhance the self rather than obscure it, inviting collaboration rather than competition, inspiration rather than reproduction. Illich offered that this is an entirely different way of thinking about personal development and about the purpose of learning and education:

> But personal growth is not a measurable entity. It is growth in disciplined dissidence, which cannot be measured against any rod, or any curriculum, nor compared to someone else's achievement. In such learning one can emulate others only in imaginative endeavor, and follow in their footsteps rather than mimic their gait. The learning I prize is immeasurable re-creation.[63]

WHO DOESN'T GET IT AT ALL?

The students in Allison's fifth-grade classroom have recently started designing and programming their own games. At the end of the previous class, Allison toured around the room, assessing students' progress with their creations. She noticed that many of their projects would benefit from the use of broadcast and receive code elements. But Allison knows from previous years that this powerful computational concept is a topic that has typically been challenging for students.

Allison begins the next day's class with an informal poll, inviting her students to reflect on their own understanding and what they need to move forward. She asks, "Alright—show of hands: Who really gets broadcast and receive?" A few students raise their hands and Allison scans the room, making eye contact and acknowledging them before moving on. Then she asks, "Who kind of gets it?" Another group of students quickly and comfortably raise their hands. Finally, Allison asks, "Who doesn't get it at all?" Without hesitation, another group of students raise their hands.

Having conducted this survey of students' understanding, Allison quickly segues into how they are going to move forward. She starts to strategically match up students based on their self-reported comfort and confidence with the broadcast and receive code elements. Pointing to one student, who indicated that they feel really comfortable with the ideas, she says, "Alright, you be with these two people," indicating two students who had shared that they were slightly less comfortable. After facilitating these matches, Allison steps back, watching as her students share their thoughts and questions, teaching each other what they know about these big ideas in their programs.

By having students publicly report their understanding and then acting on those declarations of understanding in grouping students together, Allison's goal is to help everyone develop greater capability with a core computational concept. But this strategy wouldn't work if the students didn't feel comfortable with being honest in their self-assessments. It's one matter to be quietly and privately struggling with a lack of understanding; it's quite another to confess your struggles to a large group of people.

But it's clear from Allison's question "Who doesn't get it at all?" and her students' responses that this is a classroom where students feel comfortable with not knowing. The language that Allison uses, the language that her students respond to, is straightforward and direct. It is very clear that what is being asked and expressed is about the students' assessment of their understanding, and that clarity, that lack of euphemism or obfuscation, contributes to their sense of comfort and safety. And the public declarations of understanding enable Allison to assemble groups that she thinks will best support their progress. There is an ease, a lack of friction, to the interactions portrayed here, as students encounter challenges, struggle with understanding, and continue to move forward.

In her 2000 book *Self-Theories: Their Role in Motivation, Personality, and Development,* American psychologist Carol Dweck helps us appreciate how important it is for learners to be able to encounter challenge and how special the fearless and frictionless culture of Allison's classroom is. Dweck's research was motivated by the observation that highly skilled and high-achieving students could often completely fall apart when confronted with something hard, something they didn't know or weren't able to do. As she began to explore these situations, Dweck discovered that how we respond to challenge and failure has everything to do with the theories we hold about our intelligence, about ourselves as learners and the process of learning more broadly.

Dweck identified two different ways that we might think about our intelligence: the *entity* theory of intelligence and the *incremental* theory of intelligence. From the entity viewpoint, intelligence is fixed—something we're unable to change. From the incremental viewpoint, intelligence is malleable—something we can develop with time and effort. When we hold an entity perspective on our intelligence and we encounter success, the success is affirming of how we see ourselves, as someone who is capable. But when we hold an entity perspective on our intelligence and we encounter failure, it can be perceived as determinant. The failure is a commentary about us more broadly, who we are and what we're able to accomplish. We then start to avoid failure, a fear-based response to this threat to our self-conception and our theory of intelligence. As Dweck acknowledged, this fear is understandable: "Wouldn't you be afraid of failure if each intellectual task you confronted could tell you how smart you were now and would be forever?"[64] Yet it is precisely the absence of this fear that we see reflected in Allison's classroom. Students do encounter difficulties, but there is a lack of self-protective behaviors, such as avoidance, and an absence of any shame associated with not knowing.

Dweck's research shows that while students might hold either an entity or an incremental theory of intelligence, those theories can also be changed. Allison works to purposefully create a classroom culture in which students are comfortable saying what they don't know. This is an environment where the process of learning, rather than the state of knowing, is enjoyed and exchanged. Allison contributes to this through her own constant modeling of curiosity and questioning in relationship to learning. When she encounters the unfamiliar, she is open with her students, sharing with them and encouraging experimentation, which can be heard in the language she uses with her students, such as, "I don't know how to do this" or "I haven't used this before, I'm not sure how. Why don't you go ahead and try it out?" We also see it in her decision to dedicate in-class time for students to help each other develop their understandings of coding techniques together in small groups. With this approach, Allison is focusing students' attention on learning rather than performance or success. As Dweck explained, "When children are focused on measuring themselves from their performance, failure is more likely to provoke a helpless response. When children are instead focused on learning, failure is likely to provoke continued effort."[65] And a core part of how Allison frames this learning is in terms of collective responsibility, among herself and all the students, for the understanding of everyone in the classroom. This culture makes it safe to publicly surface not knowing because it is in the service of learning and support, not competition or shame.

The classroom as design studio is necessarily replete with challenges. Students engage in open-ended work, doing things they haven't done before, inspired by what they care about, working at the edges of their competency. Sometimes, as teachers, we worry that giving students so much control and autonomy over what they make and how they make it leaves them too vulnerable: How will they feel about themselves if it doesn't work out as they wanted it to? Carol Dweck's work is a caution about the fallacy of that worry, a caution against the misguided good intentions that prompt us to want to protect the young people in our care from experiences of challenge and failure. She reminds us that the best way to support students in their emotional and cognitive development is to show them ways to meet these challenges with enthusiasm—to see them, as Allison and her students do, as opportunities to learn and grow.

WHAT DO YOU THINK?

At the beginning of the year, Katherine welcomes her high school students by inviting them to think about what a computer science classroom is. She asks them to think about what the classroom looks like, about what the people in the room are doing. Students' responses reflect stereotypes about computer science: that it's more individualistic than collaborative, more technical than creative, more scripted than exploratory. Their responses also offer Katherine a glimpse into their experiences of school more generally. Students describe learning as being told what to do and searching for right answers.

Katherine uses these responses as a jumping off point for her introduction to the year ahead. She emphasizes that what they will be doing in the classroom represents a different approach to computer science and to learning. Katherine tells the students, "I'm not lecturing. I won't be standing at the front of the room, with you at your desks. You will be getting up, looking at each other's code, helping each other with ideas, working in partners or groups to create. I will be moving around the room, ready to help, but you will be deciding what you want to create, who you will work with, and how you will iterate towards a final product. You are creating all these things yourselves. You are figuring things out yourselves." Katherine notes how this may lead to discomfort at times, that students should expect to encounter challenges and failure. She assures her students that this is part of learning, not something to be avoided or afraid of. "If you don't get it wrong," she says warmly, "you can't really grow."

Throughout the year, Katherine's students experience this new culture of learning. They create their own games and web pages, choosing what their projects will look like and figuring out how to do things they haven't done before. In her interactions with her students—whether they're discussing how to start a project, or how to fix a problem, or how they feel about what they've made—the first question Katherine usually asks them is "What do you think?"

In his provocative book *The Ignorant Schoolmaster: Five Lessons in Intellectual Emancipation*, originally published in 1987 and made available as an English translation in 1991, French philosopher Jacques Rancière shared the story of Joseph Jacotot, an exiled French teacher born in the late eighteenth century who was able to help his Flemish students learn how to read in a new language without instruction or explanation. Rancière used this historical narrative to argue for a radical reimagining of the learning process, one that fundamentally rejected what he saw in France as a positioning of the teacher as the one who knows and the students as the ones who don't. He emphasized the damage this traditional positioning does to learners' ideas about themselves, by making them think they are dependent on a teacher to have ideas.

Rancière offered two mechanisms through which teachers can free learners from dependence, enabling learners to believe in their own power and capacity. The first is to tell them directly that they don't need you to learn: "I must teach you that I have nothing to teach you."[66] The second is to create opportunities for learners to figure out for themselves what they think about something, by continually asking them, "What do you see? What do you think about it? What do you make of it?"[67] We see both of these mechanisms at work in Katherine's classroom. She is direct with her students that she is there to help them but not to tell them what to do, that they will be making decisions about what they are creating and how they will be creating it. In parallel, she is creating opportunities for them to develop their own thoughts, by asking them what they think and inviting them to create projects of their own design.

From their first moments together, Katherine makes it clear to her students that their experiences in her classroom involve a fundamentally different way of thinking about and experiencing learning. She chooses to have this conversation on the first day of class, sharing with students the ideas that guide the design of their learning experience. In Katherine's classroom, her students learn through making things they've chosen to work on, making their own ideas concrete. These ideas about learning are visible in the actions of teacher and student—they are moving in and out of interactions with others as needed, standing or sitting as invited by the work, both talking and listening. This approach also changes expectations about knowledge: who knows and what they know. By continually asking students what they think, Katherine is communicating to her students that their ideas are legitimate, that they are not just trying to guess what she or someone else has already determined. She creates an environment in which students are encouraged and expected to develop their own thoughts.

Katherine shared with us that she does this work partly in response to the ideas about computer science that her students expressed in their first class together. Some of her students weren't able to see themselves as capable of computer science; they had worries that it was too technical, too rigid, too disconnected from who they are and what they care about. But she also does this work in response to the ideas about learning her students expressed more generally, not only in computer science. Katherine hopes they will see both the original ideas for their projects and the ideas for how to improve their projects as coming from themselves, originating from their own perspectives, experiences, and interests. Rather than feeling wholly dependent on her perspective and knowledge as the teacher, she wants them to recognize their own capability and value.

Drawing on ideas about art, Rancière expressed sentiments that were very similar to Katherine's aspirations for helping her students trust themselves. Specifically, Rancière described how Jacotot invited his students to make art, and how visitors, in focusing on their own assessments of the art, often misunderstood the purpose of this activity:

> But it's not a matter of making great painters; it's a matter of making them emancipated: people capable of saying, "me too, I'm a painter," a statement that contains nothing in the way of pride, only the reasonable feeling of power that belongs to any reasonable being. . . . "Me too, I'm a painter" means: me too, I have a soul, I have feelings to communicate to my fellow-men.[68]

This is what Katherine—and every teacher who imagines their classroom as design studio—communicates to their students by inviting them to create things they care about, by inviting them to have ideas and realize them. These teachers are saying to their students: you have a soul, your thoughts and feelings matter, you have something to tell us, and we are here to listen to you.

WHAT ARE YOU GOING TO DO NOW?

Rose, a high school computer science teacher, has been working with her engineering students on programming and robotics. They've done some foundational work on input and output, sensors and actuators, looking at and experimenting with existing code. Now they are going to use those concepts in the context of a project in which they design and build their own kinetic sculptures. Addressing her students as artists and engineers, Rose invites them to immerse themselves in the work of professional kinetic artists Jean Tinguely and Arthur Ganson, and reminds them of the tools and materials they have to draw on, including a 3D printer and circuit boards. She encourages her students to think about what they want their kinetic sculpture to show or evoke and how they are going to design their sculpture to give it that particular concept or feeling.

Rose dedicates the whole next class session to concept development, creating space and time for students to imagine the sculptures they want to create—theme, aesthetic design, and technical components. Some students instantly know what they want to do. For others, it feels more challenging. One student sighs loudly and remarks to Rose, "Ugh, I don't like this. I struggle with being creative." Rose acknowledges the student's experience of uncertainty, but then encourages the student to look at what other people are doing, offering other examples of kinetic artwork and asking the student questions about their own interests and how those might be reflected in a sculpture.

As students begin the messy process of building their sculptures, they sometimes call out into the room, "It doesn't work! What am I going to do?" and "It's falling over! How do I fix that?" Rose validates their struggles, but also expresses confidence that they can develop ideas about how to move forward, responding, "Yeah, it doesn't work. What are you going to do now?"

The sculptures the students create through this process reflect powerful ideas from the disciplines of engineering and art, while simultaneously being meaningfully connected to their own personalities and interests. One student has a hard time coming up with an idea, and picks an existing sculpture that they enjoyed and appreciated, using a circuit board to power its reimagining. Another student reflects on artworks that they love and decides to make a sculpture of Vincent van Gogh's *Starry Night* with moving elements. One student makes an ocean scene to reflect their enthusiasm for marine animals. And another makes a clock that doesn't run at a regular speed, with hands sometimes spinning around quickly and sometimes slowly, to illustrate their perceptual experience of time as a senior in high school.

When Rose spoke with us about her interactions with learners during this project, she used the term "moral support" to describe what she was doing. She responds to learners in their moments of challenge, but without directing them or telling them what to do. The interactions she has with learners prompt them back to their own ideas, and to their sense of themselves as people who can figure things out. Rose placed these interactions within the broader context of her aspirations for student learning, summarizing what she felt was most important:

> Students having agency and autonomy in the classroom. That it's not about me, as the teacher. I'm there to support their development rather than be the authority in the classroom. I'm there to provide the underlying knowledge—and support that development and support their working through projects. But it's about what they're doing in the classroom.

When Rose asks her students, "What are you going to do now?," she is communicating to them her belief in their agency and autonomy. She is helping them think through what they might do next in the work, a reassuring reminder that they have ways to move forward and enact their ideas, even when it seems difficult.

American science educator and philosopher David Hawkins offered the word *respect* to describe the particular nature of the kinds of interactions we see between teachers and their students in the classroom as design studio. As exemplified by Rose and her students, these interactions offer support but in the context of foregrounding learners' relationships to their own ideas and efforts to enact them. As Hawkins wrote in a 1967 essay, entitled "I, Thou, It":

> The more basic gift is not love but respect, respect for others as ends in themselves, as actual and potential artisans of their own learnings and doings, of their own lives. . . . Respect for the young is not a passive, hands-off attitude. It invites our own offering of resources, it moves us toward the furtherance of their lives.[69]

We tend to see this expression of respect for learners most obviously in moments when they are struggling. Hawkins noted that there can be moments in classrooms when learners are so engaged in the interesting work in front of them—the projects that teachers like Rose have purposefully designed to create just that experience—that it can seem like the teacher could leave the room and no one would notice. But, just because learners don't always need adult intervention doesn't mean that they don't sometimes need it very much. Rose's words and actions are essential to fostering her learners' sense of capacity for self-directedness and self-expression, which in turn helps learners make their ideas real, which in turn helps them understand themselves as people capable of self-direction and self-expression. As Hawkins wrote, "No child, I wish to say, can gain competence and knowledge, or know himself as competent and as a knower, save through communication with others involved with him in his enterprises."[70]

Rose spoke with us about coming to a similar realization in her own teaching. She had become increasingly conscious of her "one-on-one interactions with students and the impact of what I am saying to them in the moment," as being separate from but as important as her work in setting up the projects, realizing that the selection of content and design of assignments alone couldn't always help learners engage with the ideas and advance their understanding. Rose attributed this new consciousness to a colleague's recent observation of Rose's interactions with some students who were struggling with a project. The colleague had noted how important it was that Rose had acknowledged they were struggling, offered some framing of why the task was so hard, and used that as a jumping-off point for inviting the students to think about what they might want to do in response. Having this experience reflected back to her by a colleague prompted Rose to reflect on, as she described, "how important it is to name that struggle out loud, name the problem for the student, and validate the feelings in the moment." It gave her greater awareness of how she was helping students work through the challenges that confronted them, supporting them as competent and autonomous thinkers.

The "I, Thou, It" of Hawkins's title referred to the intersecting relationships of student, teacher, and content in the learning environment. Hawkins was concerned not only with the significance of the teacher's impact on the development of students' ideas and understanding, as described earlier, but also with the significance of content on the interactions between students and teachers. Teachers cannot respect students as people with ideas absent a learning environment in which they can actually have ideas, in which there are materials (both intellectual and physical) for them to work with, explore, and create. As Hawkins wrote:

> We must provide for children those kinds of environments which elicit their interests and talents and which deepen their engagement in practice and thought. An environment of "loving" adults who are themselves alienated from the world around them is an educational vacuum. Adults involved in the world of man and nature bring that world with them to children, bounded and made safe to be sure, but not thereby losing its richness and promise of novelty. It was this emphasis which made me insist upon the third pronoun in the title, the impersonal "It" alongside the "I" and "Thou." Adults and children, like adults with each other, can associate well only in worthy interests and pursuits.[71]

This is what we see in Rose's classroom. The kinetic sculpture project invites learners into a rich world of ideas, engaging with the inspiring creations of professional artists, their own nascent technical competencies, and their own interests and personalities. We see evidence of this opportunity, this engagement with the world in the descriptions of the sculptures that Rose's students have made, as they use their interests as a way into making something aesthetically and technically compelling. Rose can ask them about what they want their sculpture to show, about what they are going to do in the face of a collapsing structure, because there is substance there from which to develop a response. Within their projects they can actually be, in Hawkins's words, the "artisans of their own learnings and doings."[72]

WHAT CAN YOU MAKE WITH IT?

Middle school librarian and media specialist Ana's seventh graders are starting a new project. They'll each choose a programming language and learn to create something with it. "What can you do with it? What can you make with it?" she prompts them, going on to explain, "The goal isn't for you to become an expert coder, but to begin to understand how programming works so you can get the computer to do what you want. I'm not telling you what to make because each coding language has its own use. Some of you are going to make games, some of you are going to make websites. You have your own ideas."

Some students are initially skeptical that they will be able to figure things out for themselves. Ana helps connect them with resources, reminding them of informational videos online and the expertise of their own classmates. When a student, after looking at a website as a resource for their own program, asks, "Can I just copy this code?" Ana reminds the student that they are learning what they need for their own purposes, saying, "Yeah, the basic code you can copy. But you have to make it work for what you're doing." Other students need support in having confidence in their own ideas and discovering what they care about. One student has chosen to learn a popular text-based programming language, but isn't feeling engaged by their project. Ana suggests a pivot, saying, "If you don't like what you're doing, then why are you doing it?" and encourages them to try something else if they aren't happy.

As students get deeper into the work, Ana sees how her students are able to get the languages they've selected to work for their creative goals. They also seem to be more focused and self-sufficient in their technical problem-solving. Ana notices that rather than calling her over to say that they are stuck or don't understand the coding language they are working with, students are calling her over in excitement to share what they've made and figured out. They call out to her across the room or catch her as she is going by, saying: "Come play my game! Come see my robot! Watch this!"

This choose-your-own-coding-language project wasn't the first way that Ana tried to help her students learn to code. She shared her initial experience of helping students engage in programming, when she had students learn web development by moving through structured, progressive lessons from a preexisting curriculum. She felt as though she had to clearly see the inputs and outcomes of their learning to code, that she had to "hold on to control." But this method, with everyone learning in the same way, doing the same thing, didn't work—for anyone. Everyone, including Ana, was frustrated. "I hated it," she says. "They hated every last minute of it. It wasn't important to them. They didn't feel invested in it." Frustrated by her own and the students' lack of excitement, enjoyment, and meaningful connection to learning, Ana decided to make a radical change and designed this more student-directed project.

In this project, Ana is inviting her students into an entirely different relationship to learning. It isn't about learning a programming language for its own sake or performing to an externally defined standard of proficiency. Instead, Ana is helping students see that code is something they can use in the service of their own goals and desires, that those goals can and should drive what they learn (by choosing the coding language that best meets the needs of their project) and how they learn (by selecting the resources to best support their work). In our conversations with her, Ana drew on her own experience and identity as an artist to articulate the kind of relationship she wanted her students to have to coding—one in which they were determining what it would be used for, in which it was a tool for their self-expression. She explained:

> I'm an artist and I always thought of coding as boring. But then I realized all these cool things I can do with it and make it do what I want. I see it more now as an artistic medium than a boring dry thing. So that's one of the things I want them to get out of it—this is a paintbrush and palette, this is clay. You've got to make it work for you, and make it relate to you, too.

She leads with "What can you make with it?" as a framing question, to help her students focus on the importance of their own ideas, which in turn will help them choose a coding language to express those ideas. She provides resources that foreground the learners' own agency, helping them see that what is important isn't the specifics of what they learn but what they want to use it for. She continually reminds students that their excitement for what they are creating is core to learning, and that its absence is a signal to do something different.

Canadian scientist Ursula Franklin offered us language to understand the significance of the shift that Ana describes here, moving from prescriptive lessons to a choose-your-own-language coding project, and what the shift embodies as a way of thinking about coding, and a way of thinking about learning. In a series of lectures given for Canadian public radio in 1989 titled *The Real World of Technology*, Franklin asserted that technology is not just a set of tools or materials, it is a practice, a way of doing things. She argued there is danger when a tool that is used to accomplish a particular goal comes to be seen as the only way to do something, as the one right way to do it.

Franklin offered a set of contrasting metaphors to understand the difference: a *production* model and a *growth* model. In a production model, the focus is on control, on a predictable system of inputs and outputs, and what is being made and how does not change in response to the individuals doing the making or the context in which it is being made. Franklin contrasted this with a growth model, explaining:

> Growth itself cannot be commandeered; it can only be nurtured and encouraged by providing a suitable environment. Growth occurs; it is not made. Within a growth model, all that human intervention can do is to try to discover the best conditions for growth and try to meet them. In any given environment, the growing organism develops at its own rate. . . . There is something comforting in a production model—everything seems in hand, nothing is left to chance—while growth is always chancy.[73]

Franklin argued that education is the clearest illustration of a growth activity, yet one that is increasingly forced into a production model. Students are increasingly being treated as the same; schools are increasingly expected to produce predictable, measurable results of learning. Behind this control is a legitimate worry, that students won't learn in ways they need. But that control itself is counterproductive to learning because it does not enable learners to find meaning in their work, and it does not enable teachers to change in response to the real experiences of the individuals in their classrooms.

Ana acknowledged that in designing this project she was embracing this chanciness, "throwing everything out the window." The freedom afforded students in this approach resulted in uncertainty of what they would make, uncertainty about the exact nature of the coding knowledge they would emerge with. She shared how colleagues would respond with skepticism when her answer to their question of "How are you teaching coding?" was "However the kids want to learn coding." She remarked, "It scares people. It scared me."

In the classroom as design studio, learning involves an embrace of uncertainty, and so, too, does teaching. It is not only that Ana was thinking about her students' learning as a growth model, but also that she was engaging with her own teaching in a similar way—thinking about the range of tools and activities at her disposal and how they might best support her ideas for what she wanted to do. If we as teachers are to foster the kind of growth that Franklin called for, that Ana's students experienced through this project, then we also must be supported in making decisions and judgments that might scare us, as we respond to the needs of the unique individuals in our classrooms, trying new things even when we do not know how they will work out.

HOW CAN WE FIX IT?

Across Penny's four middle school computer classes, students are designing and programming math-themed games. Some students are creating games to help the player practice a particular mathematical skill; some students are building tutorials to help the user understand a specific mathematical concept. To help keep track of student progress, Penny has created an online gallery space where students can share their projects as they are being developed.

Penny calls their shared virtual space the *Debugging Studio* because she wants students to feel comfortable sharing projects that maybe aren't yet working as they envisioned. One advantage to this public sharing of buggy projects is that students across the four classes are able to help each other by trying out each other's projects, documenting bugs, and making suggestions for possible solutions. In class, Penny invites her students to each pick a project from the Debugging Studio and figure out what's happening with it. She reminds her students of their goal with their selected project by asking, "How can we fix it?"

As Penny walks around the room, she sees how engrossed students are in others' projects. Students have documents open to record their observations and feedback as they work to discover bugs in the code. They find a variety of bugs in each other's programs: a multiplication error, a typo in output text, a button that doesn't respond when clicked.

The debugging work is accompanied by appreciation. One student admiringly points out especially complex code to Penny, while another student demonstrates a project they think is especially wonderful: "Look at how cool this is!" At the end of the session, Penny helps students share their feedback with the project's original programmer, offering their admiration and their ideas for how to fix bugs in the project.

By naming the work of debugging as central to their processes of creation, Penny is inviting her students into a particular relationship to learning, one characterized by trying and fixing and trying again. In his 1980 book *Mindstorms*, South African-born mathematician, computer scientist, and educator Seymour Papert, who was mentored by Jean Piaget and co-created the Logo programming language, described the opportunity that programming work provides for this relationship to learning, and the idea of debugging as an alternative to the destructive fear of failure that can dominate learning situations framed around being right or wrong:

> Many children are held back in their learning because they have a model of learning in which you have either "got it" or "got it wrong." But when you learn to program a computer you almost never get it right the first time. Learning to be a master programmer is learning to become highly skilled at isolating and correcting "bugs," the parts that keep the program from working. The question to ask about the program is not whether it is right or wrong, but if it is fixable. If this way of looking at intellectual products were generalized to how the larger culture thinks about knowledge and its acquisition, we all might be less intimidated by our fears of "being wrong."[74]

While the concept of debugging originated with programming work, Papert was interested in broader ways of thinking about learning. In the classroom as design studio, the process of creating through projects is necessarily messy and iterative. There will always be surprises as creators take their ideas from conception to implementation. What can make this messy, iterative, and surprising process joyful in the classroom—rather than stressful or shameful—are the dual elements of the classroom culture that Penny creates here, where bugs are normal and expected parts of creation and there is a collective commitment to working together to fix them.

In this vignette from Penny's classroom, we see the commitment to a culture of fixing, rather than being right or wrong, being enacted at multiple levels: students being invited to share their own buggy projects in need of fixing and students being invited to help fix others' projects. By creating a shared studio, Penny has introduced a low-stakes way for her students to easily share their projects with each other when they are ready for help and feedback. And by establishing a simple protocol of tracking bugs through text documents, Penny also makes it easy for her students to review each other's code and work through feedback. These straightforward elements of classroom procedure normalize the idea that students will encounter difficulties, that things won't work the first time around, and, through making the process of debugging public and collective, everyone is invited into a shared responsibility for trying to make things better.

In addition, in her own behavior, Penny serves as a powerful model of learning by trying to fix things, rather than worrying about getting it wrong. Papert noted that one of the most important influences on children's way of thinking about learning in a given subject is how they are initiated, explicitly or implicitly, into that subject by adults. For example, if adults themselves seem scared of mathematical problems and reluctant to engage with them, young people will do the same. If adults are instead excited to meet a challenge, willing to try without the guarantee of success, and interested in what that experience might teach them, young people have both a model of how they can engage and permission to fail.

Papert highlighted how powerful it can be when teachers and students experience not knowing together. He described as "poignant" a scene with a small group of fifth graders who were working on a Logo project together, programming a mechanical turtle to write out a seasonal greeting. When the turtle ran the program, a bug emerged and the teacher and one of her students sat together for some debugging. Reflecting on their interaction, Papert wrote:

> As they puzzled together the child had a revelation: "Do you mean," he said, "that you really don't know how to fix it?" The child did not yet know how to say it, but what had been revealed to him was that he and the teacher had been engaged together in a research project.[75]

In Penny's class, students routinely experience the "revelation" that Papert described: the realization that a teacher genuinely doesn't know something and is excited to figure it out alongside you.

In her classroom, Penny joins her students in their experiences of debugging with interest and enthusiasm. As she shared with us, "I must tell you I still do like to chew on a nice computer problem." Penny went on to describe a time when a student came to her with a bug in the random variable generator he had created. They sat down together and worked through the program, noticing that it was telling the player they had given an incorrect answer to an addition question when the answer had actually been correct. They worked together to isolate the problem, trying different things such as attempting to produce a correct answer and seeing what had happened with the variables, before finally identifying that the issue was with the number of variables being used and how they were being used. The time Penny takes with this student, the depth of her engagement with the problem, and her curiosity and joy in figuring it out communicate important messages about learning. As Papert explained:

> School teaches that errors are bad; the last thing one wants to do is pore over them, dwell on them, or think about them. The child is glad to take advantage of the computer's ability to erase it all without any trace for anyone to see. The debugging philosophy suggests an opposite attitude. Errors benefit us because they lead us to study what happened, to understand what went wrong, and, through understanding, to fix it.[76]

In this moment, Penny is helping her students do exactly what Papert named as both difficult and essential, using errors as an opportunity for reflection and learning by dwelling on them rather than erasing them, relishing them rather than running away from them.

Many of the descriptions of debugging in Papert's *Mindstorms* are similar to this moment, made up of individuals and pairs, both student-student and student-teacher. But there is something especially significant about the collective engagement with debugging in Penny's classroom that she invites through her creation of the Debugging Studio. By distributing debugging responsibility among her students, Penny has made it possible for her students to get feedback on their projects more quickly. And the feedback students generated offered greater detail because they had time to thoroughly explore each project beyond what Penny would have been able to produce on her own for her more than one hundred students. But as powerful as the learning was for students through receiving responsive and deep feedback, students also benefited from engaging in the work of fixing others' projects and preparing feedback in support of that work. In addition to giving them some needed distance from the complexities of their own projects, students had the opportunity to practice problem-solving in novel contexts with other students' code. And, reading others' code and interacting with others' projects often served as inspiration for new creative possibilities. As Penny explained, "I think encouraging the students to interact with the creative content of others builds their own creative talents. It also leads to conversations about things that were well-done and perhaps a bit unusual as the students had very different ways of designing and building their programs." In the work of the design studio, the community context of creation means that all students are simultaneously creators and receivers of work, learning in both roles.

Penny acknowledged that her own experiences as a computer programmer prior to entering teaching certainly informed her embrace of debugging in the classroom. But, it was the orientation to learning embodied by this practice that was most important to her in her teaching. In describing to us her own iterative process as a teacher, especially her willingness to try new things (more open-ended projects, more student ownership over assessment), she emphasized letting go of the fear of failure, just as she encouraged her students to do. As she shared, "Well, really, what's the worst that could happen, right? The worst that could happen is we have to redo it. And okay, then we'll redo it and we'll come up with a different way." This is what Papert invites us into, debugging not just as a programming practice, but as an approach to learning, an approach to life. For both students and teachers in the classroom as design studio, all we can do is try, take what has gone awry as an opportunity to learn, and ask, with interest, excitement, and optimism: "How can we fix it?"

DOES ANYONE WANT TO SHARE?

Toward the end of most classes in Jordan's elementary STEAM lab, he usually asks his students, "Does anyone want to share?" Some students, right in the middle of a task they are trying to complete, remark, "Nope. Still working!" Others respond, "Oh! I want to share," and send Jordan the game they have been coding to be projected on the screen at the front of the room. Students gather around the screen, asking each other questions about the work in progress that is being shared and generating ideas for things to potentially try during their next session together.

On a chilly day in December, Jordan's students prepare for what he calls a *mini-showcase*. A distinguishing element of this showcase is that it is purposefully for works in progress, not finished products. Students from across the grades he teaches are gathering together to share some of their current project work. Not only will learners have the opportunity to show their work to students in other classes, but outside guests will also be in attendance, including the school principal, a teacher from another school, a technology coordinator, and local researchers. As students move throughout the room—gathering the material for their projects and looking at what others have done—the energy in the room is informal but also charged with excitement.

As learners present, they explain not only what they have done but also where they are taking the work next, what they still want to do and figure out. Two students are coding a dress-up game. They are in the middle of figuring out how to integrate a new feature, a Done button, and explain how they're thinking about the new feature: "We're going to change it so that all of the other clothing items disappear when you click on the button that shows you're done." Another student presents the stop-motion animation project that her group is working on. She explains that she still needs to upload the images from camera to computer, and then figure out how to edit them to create a coherent animation. Two other students have made a poster about the places they were born, the Dominican Republic and Puerto Rico, including images of each location's flag and other cultural symbols. They explain their plans to use copper tape connected to a sensor so that when a visual element on the poster is touched, the digital project will offer the viewer information about what the element represents. Across the room, one student who has made an interactive collage calls out to a visitor before her presentation, "You're going to take notes, right?"

The project showcase is a well-established pedagogical strategy. It is a way to celebrate accomplishment and honor achievement, and an opportunity for learners to display their creations for an appreciative audience. But when a showcase focuses on final products, it can also sometimes be stressful and anxiety-inducing, emphasizing polished and finished work in ways that may be misaligned with what learners actually need. By looking at what has been done without also considering what learners might create and learn next, it may also miss out on the potential benefits of meaningfully contributing to the development of work. A final project showcase can unintentionally risk communicating that it is only worth celebrating and recognizing endpoints.

When Jordan spoke with us about why he had organized the showcase to emphasize works in progress, building on his daily, in-class ritual of asking "Does anyone want to share?," he noted how valuable it was for students' learning to present their work before it was finished, and to get responses from a variety of others at early stages. "I think as we talk about things we've created, we get more excited, and then it makes us want to keep doing it and maybe making something we made better and expand on it," Jordan explained. "Allowing others to come in during the projects, tasks, and assignments allows students to get feedback and prompting from various voices to get them thinking and enhance an original idea." Jordan's thinking about the work-in-progress showcase is rooted in his commitment to supporting future learning.

Jordan's students can benefit from this special opportunity to share in the showcase in multiple ways. First, the showcase environment provides a platform for sharing what they care about and what matters to them. It is a venue where learners develop excitement around their ideas and motivation to enact them, which we saw in the energy of the showcase Jordan organized. His students also benefit from having an audience—a source of new ideas and energy to help them further develop their work. The showcase brings in the multiple perspectives of the audience members at a moment when they can be most useful, when their feedback and responses can help learners develop their ideas further. And finally, the focus on works in progress—a strategy to potentially reduce the performance anxiety that students may experience during final presentations—underscores the power of process and iteration, encouraging risk-taking and experimentation in a lower-stakes environment.

What is important to Jordan here, and what we see as essential to the classroom as design studio more generally, is an interest and engagement with what has yet to be created and what has yet to be learned—a sentiment echoed by American educational philosopher John Dewey, who argued that the central purpose of education is fostering a "desire to go on learning."[77] In his 1938 book *Experience and Education*, Dewey explored the importance and value of learning experiences that connected young people to the world and its myriad possibilities, and built upon their inclinations toward curiosity and exploration. He expressed concern about school experiences in which learning was effectively reduced to the collection and regurgitation of facts, an experience of learning that might inevitably lead students to be "rendered callous to ideas."[78] As Dewey wrote:

> What avail is it to win prescribed amounts of information about geography and history, to win ability to read and write, if in the process the individual loses his own soul: loses his appreciation of the things worth while, of the values to which these things are relative; if he loses desire to apply what he has learned and, above all, the ability to extract meaning from his future experiences as they occur?[79]

In Jordan's classroom, students are invited to share in the showcase not only to celebrate what they have already done, but also to explore what is to come, to prepare for the future experiences Dewey referred to, fueled by their personal investment in their projects and the opportunity to talk with others about ideas that matter to them.

By framing the showcase around works in progress, Jordan is inviting both learners and audience to attend to the process of development and its implications for future learning, rather than evaluation of the project as product. He encourages his students to see the audience as valuable to their future learning, receiving feedback and ideas to help them figure out what they want and could do, as illustrated by the student calling out to make sure a visitor is going to take notes that they can share afterward. As suggested in the preceding Dewey quote, educational experiences that are forward-looking, that support the desire to learn more, invite different kinds of relationships among learners than educational experiences that focus on performance of accumulated knowledge, on competition over collaboration. A collaborative spirit permeates the daily environment of Jordan's room, reflected in the comfort and enthusiasm with which learners share their work in progress as part of day-to-day interactions: leaning over to ask for help with a bug or line of code, or proudly displaying a recent discovery or emergent creation.

The value of work in progress as a learning opportunity is often underappreciated in educational environments, and there are multiple forces that can instead pull teachers and students back toward the focus on accumulation and performance of knowledge that Dewey cautioned against. In organizing this particular showcase around sharing works in progress, or in asking his students at the end of an ordinary class, "Does anyone want to share?," Jordan is proactively working to foster a different culture of learning—one that helps his students embrace curiosity over accomplishment, and helps them think about learning as a never-ending process. Through his recognition and celebration of works in progress, Jordan is creating the conditions that encourage and enable learners to think for themselves about the next steps in their work, what they might be able to do, and what the future might hold.

WHO DISCOVERED THE COOLEST THINGS?

The fourth graders in Kelly's STEAM lab have begun making digital museums about themselves. They create backdrops showing four objects that they've selected to represent their personalities and their interests, and then design a character that acts as a tour guide walking a visitor through the gallery, telling them about each object and its importance. Kelly has purposefully arranged the students in groups to create opportunities for learners to interact with those around them and to talk about what they are doing. Students excitedly point to one another's screens, or get up out of their seats to gather around someone else's project.

Ideas pass quickly from one student to another. One group focuses on the idea of drawing backgrounds rather than finding them in the program. They create museum facades with dazzling ombré effects, blending purple and rainbow hues. After this shared experimenting, their projects quickly diverge, with each student finding their own way. At another table, after the students have figured out their four museum objects, they each go on to focus on different aspects of their projects; some create sound effects, while others script the dialogue that will accompany their animations. At one table a group of students spend a long period of time discussing ways to change the color of a character, with each student deciding to take a different approach: "Well, I'm drawing it." "I'm recoloring the whole thing." "I'm going to use the fill." At another table students discuss how to transition from one scene to another, with some of them using arrow keys and others using sensors.

As the students work, Kelly circulates from table to table, helping to turn all of these discoveries into a collective resource. She excitedly calls out what someone has done: "Oh wow! He's stamping himself into a kaleidoscope! That's really cool." As she arrives at each table, she asks, "Okay, who discovered the coolest things?" She looks at who everyone is pointing to, but has other students at the table tell her about the discovery and how it worked. As time for the project comes to a close that day, she pulls together a list of the discoveries that the students shared. She presents each discovery back to the whole group, asking if anyone can find a different way to produce a similar effect. After someone offers an idea, she prompts her students again to suggest another way. The class responds with excitement, gaining in their confidence with programming as they figure out their own strategies and preferences for how to do things.

In the classroom as design studio, learners express themselves not only in what they make, but in how they make it. The students in Kelly's classroom are creating projects that reflect themselves, but their processes of doing so—what they focus on and how they engage with the technical environment—also reflect something of themselves. Different students take on certain kinds of tasks earlier than others, with some focusing on establishing the visual layout and others focusing on what will be said. The technical implementations of their programs, how their programs work, are also spaces where learners can engage in different ways of thinking, doing, and being. When a student declares that they will accomplish a transition with sensors while another is using arrow keys, or when a student asserts that they want to draw their own sprite rather than recolor an existing one, they are asserting themselves in the work, conscious of what their classmates are doing but still exploring their own methods and processes. Kelly's classroom practices are supportive of this diversity of approaches. She expresses interest and enthusiasm for individuals' unique methods of figuring out how to do things.

An article from 1990 by MIT-based sociologist and psychologist Sherry Turkle and computer scientist Seymour Papert, "Epistemological Pluralism: Styles and Voices within the Computer Culture," helps us appreciate the importance of what Kelly is supporting in her classroom. Drawing on their research with both college students and elementary students learning programming, Turkle and Papert were excited by the promise of the computer as an expressive medium, to be used by individuals to realize their own ideas with their own methods—as Kelly's students do here. Turkle and Papert saw the computer's potential for supporting an *epistemological pluralism*, or "the validity of multiple ways of knowing and thinking."[80]

But, they argued, the potential of a tool, like the computer, could be diminished by the surrounding culture in which it is used. It doesn't matter if a computer can support multiple ways of knowing and thinking if the setting in which it is used doesn't honor that multiplicity. Turkle and Papert outlined the ways in which formal and abstract thinking had crowded out other ways of knowing and being. Using an introductory computer science course at Harvard as an example, they described the experiences of two students, Lisa and Robin, who approach their programming in more concrete and experimental ways, wanting to play with and understand the details, rather than engaging in abstract or planning-oriented methods. Turkle and Papert related how Lisa and Robin were successful in their work, but were discouraged in pursuing their work using methods that felt more comfortable to them:

> Lisa's and Robin's experiences make it clear that the computer can be a partner in a great diversity of relationships, that the computer is an expressive medium that different people can make their own in their own way. Yet those who wish to approach the computer in a noncanonical way are discouraged by the dominant computer culture, eloquently expressed in the ideology of the Harvard University course. They are asked to change their style to suit the fashion when they begin to interact with the official computer world, committed to a formal, rule-driven, hierarchical approach to programming. Like Lisa and Robin, their exclusion from the computer culture is perpetuated not by rules that keep them out, but by ways of thinking that make them reluctant to join in.[81]

Their ways of learning were not valued, and, in turn, Lisa and Robin lost interest, not being able to see themselves in the work, feeling as though programming and computers were not for them. They began to distrust their own instincts and inclinations, withdrawing into a rote proceduralism, disconnected from the joy of discovery and creation experienced by Kelly's students.

Resonant with what Turkle and Papert cautioned about the hazards of thinking there is one "right" way to do programming, Kelly expressed a similar concern about the culture of education more broadly, describing how learners would ask her if they should do things "like this?," reflecting a worry that they were diverging from a presumed correct path. To these types of student inquiries, she would respond encouragingly and affirmatively: "Like you want. Any way you want." Kelly went on to describe her own motivation in wanting her students to feel seen and validated for who they were, what they had to say, and how they thought about things—and how much she sought to design work that enabled them to see those things in themselves.

> I want them to see that creative computing is really just a giant microphone. It is a way to amplify their voice and their imagination. And that their voice, their ideas, and what they make are worthy of being seen and heard. That's what I want them to take away from here.

It is precisely this feeling, of seeing programming as an extension of their voice, and thus a space where they can find their own way of doing it, that we see reflected in the idea of epistemological pluralism.

But Kelly is doing more than helping her students figure out their own approaches to programming. She is making those differences visible, and in ways that contribute to a deeply collaborative, rather than competitive, classroom culture. As Turkle and Papert warned, the surfacing of difference in methods and styles does not necessarily lead to pluralism—it can instead lead to competition. In Kelly's classroom, the idea that there are multiple, equally valid and legitimate paths to accomplishing something is a central tenet. Kelly communicates this belief through the language that she uses with her students, by encouraging them to do their work in any way they want, defending against the devaluing of their own ideas that she fears they have absorbed in educational experiences structured around the idea that there is one right answer. She also communicates this belief through her classroom practices around celebrating individual approaches to figuring things out, inviting students to recognize what others have discovered, and foregrounding the existence and value of multiple approaches. Her question directed to one group of students—"Who discovered the coolest things?"—is not an invitation to competition, as it might be under other circumstances, but instead an invitation to celebrate and admire individuality and multiplicity. Her students' responses demonstrate how they have internalized this sense of epistemological pluralism, as they listen with curiosity and excitement to what others have done and then declare with enthusiasm and confidence how they are going to continue on their own paths.

WHAT ARE OTHER PEOPLE DOING?

Jordan's elementary STEAM classroom thrums with voices and activity as students work on their programming projects. Students are continually moving around the room and interacting with each other: swapping headphones to listen to each other's audio selections, leaning across the table to peek at what a neighbor is doing, gathering excitedly around a computer to play-test a project. In the midst of these interactions, students are constantly making discoveries. One student has added a funny sound to their project, another has figured out how to separate the different parts of a sprite, and another has created multiple copies of an image. One student calls out to another, "Come see what I made!" After a long struggle, another student proudly calls out, "Yes! I've got it!" Classmates run over in both appreciation and curiosity, excited to see what's been figured out.

Jordan has organized the physical space of his classroom to support interaction among these many different project trajectories, offering students varied configurations of surfaces and seats to work from. Two students collaborating on a project happily spread out on a front table. Another student is standing by the radiator with her computer on the windowsill, and is soon joined by a classmate looking for inspiration and advice. Jordan has set up a large coordinate grid on a wall in the classroom and students periodically get up out of their seats to act out the movement along the x and y coordinates to better understand the directions they are coding in their projects.

The coordinate grid wall is one of many places where learners gather to ask each other and Jordan questions, sharing things that aren't working out as they might have intended and looking for resources and advice. Jordan also keeps an eye out for students who might be silently struggling, perhaps in need of additional support. Spotting a student across the room stuck in struggle and not making progress, Jordan gently reminds the student of the resources in the room, encouraging the student, "Just close your computer. Take a walk around the room. What are other people doing?"

In Jordan's classroom, learners are doing things their own way—in what they create and in how they work, interact, and use the physical space. When we spoke with Jordan about what he most valued about the learning in his classroom, he focused on stories of individual students, their growth and their hard-won successes. He described two students who persisted with a project throughout an entire class period, whereas a few months ago they would have given up part way through and moved on to something else. "That was huge for them," he noted enthusiastically. He explained how remarkable it was that another student was able to casually ask him questions about the work, and use the responses to make adjustments to his own project, after initially being hesitant and embarrassed about asking for help. He shared the recent experiences of an unenthusiastic and disconnected eighth grader, who found interest in designing a cityscape and building her own electrical stop light, declaring at the end of the project, "I'm actually proud of this."

Jordan connected his focus on learners as individuals to his past work as a special education teacher, describing himself as a "SPED teacher for life." He had been frustrated as a general education teacher by the sense that there was too often only "one way to do it" for students in classroom learning experiences, when students need many ways to do things, responsive to their needs and interests. Now as a STEAM teacher, he felt there were new opportunities. "When I got into this role here, I'm like, I'm done with that. Because I know kids can do a lot more. They're capable of a lot more than what the regular classroom restricts them to."

With their concept of "culture *as* disability," anthropologists and educators Ray McDermott and Hervé Varenne give us a way of making sense of the enabling or constraining dimensions of the classroom that Jordan describes. Rather than being objective realities, experiences of ability and disability, of competence and incompetence, of inclusion and exclusion are instead socially constructed. As they explained in their 1995 article "Culture *as* Disability":

> People use established cultural forms to define what they should work on, work for, in what way, and with what consequences; being in a culture is a great occasion for developing abilities, or at least for having many people think they have abilities. People also use established cultural forms to define those who do not work on the "right" things, for the "right" reason, or in the "right" way. Being in a culture is a great occasion for developing disabilities, or at least for having many people think that they have disabilities. . . . People in all cultures can use established cultural forms to disable each other. By established cultural forms, we mean anything from built physical structures that leave people locked out of public places, through bad school assessment systems that leave people from learning what is in some way needed, on to metaphors and tropes that deliver so consistently a view of people as less than they are.[82]

Jordan's attention to learners' individuality, his continually responsive, thoughtful structuring of opportunities for them to learn and create, reflect his aspiration for the classroom to be fundamentally enabling, rather than disabling. His approach to talking about learners and what they are able to do rejects ideas of "normal" and "typical," instead focusing on the possibilities of open-ended, student-directed project work to honor young people's own ways of doing things. His stories about learners' personal growth are portraits of individuals coming to see themselves as competent and capable through their own creations, not through someone else's definition for them of what those labels mean. And through his creation of spaces in which learners feel safe naming the struggles that inevitably arise during the navigation of such open-ended work (such as the impromptu meeting space at the coordinate grid), feelings of competence are not threatened by experiences of challenge and difficulty.

All of this individual action and exploration is enabled by, and enables, connections with others. As McDermott and Varenne wrote:

> The coherence of any culture is not given by members being the same, nor by members knowing the same things. Instead, the coherence of a culture is crafted from the partial and mutually dependent knowledge of each person caught in the process and depends, in the long run, on the work they do together. Life in culture . . . is polyphonous and multivocalic; it is made of the voices of many, each one brought to life and made significant by the others, only sometimes being the same, more often by being different, more dramatically by being contradictory.[83]

In Jordan's classes, students are excited to share their differences, to show others what they've done, and their peers respond with interest and curiosity when they encounter the many ways of doing things. Differences in what students have done and how they did it are not a source of shame but instead an opportunity to learn. When Jordan asks his students, "What are other people doing?," he is not using the question as a way of comparing students or pressuring students to conform, as this question might be used in other contexts. Instead, it is an invitation to look to others as inspiration and resources in figuring out your own ideas. In the classroom as design studio, differences are a source of strength.

DID YOU ASK YOUR NEIGHBOR?

Next to each student's computer in Tonya's middle school STEAM classroom, you'll find a set of red and green cups. If things are going smoothly enough for a student while they're working, they display their green cup. But if a student runs into problems, they swap out their green cup for their red cup.

Every class, starting at the beginning of the school year, Tonya encourages her students to use the cups to share with others in the room how they are currently doing. She reminds them that it's valuable to communicate where they are with their work and what they need, and to reach out to others for support as needed. When she starts seeing red cups in the room, suggesting that students might be stuck and in need of help, she calls out, "Did you ask your neighbor? Did you ask your other neighbor? Did you ask that neighbor that's on the other side of them?"

Tonya stops by one student's computer, where the student is working on programming a video game. She listens carefully to the student as they describe their current problem with variables. After a pause, Tonya says, "I don't know the answer, but I'll go look it up and report back." As she continues working her way around the room, another student asks for help. After listening to this student, she realizes there's an opportunity for connection. She calls out to another classmate, "Hey, you figured this out. Can you come over and explain to us and show us what you did?" After connecting those two learners, she resumes her walk and stops at another student. The student is experiencing some unanticipated behavior with a sprite in their project. Curious, Tonya pulls up a chair and sits with the student. "I don't know what's going on," she says, "but we can try to figure it out together."

The classroom as design studio is a space of individual development, learning, and creation, situated in a community of learners, including the teacher as learner. We see this in action in Tonya's classroom: she has designed the learning environment to foreground the community of learners as a resource for their own learning. In her 1990 book *Apprenticeship in Thinking: Cognitive Development in Social Context,* American psychologist Barbara Rogoff offered the powerful language of *guided participation* to describe this learning. Through her cross-cultural studies of children's learning in a variety of contexts, from home and classrooms and beyond, Rogoff theorized and demonstrated how learning is an active, social process. Children learn by participating in problem-solving and culturally relevant activities, supported by others—guided by peers and by more expert others, such as caregivers, parents, and teachers. While acknowledging the value of the structured support adults can offer, she recognized the varied, unique, and important contributions that peers can offer each other in their learning and development:

> Peers may be less skilled partners than adults in some activities, but may offer unique possibilities for discussion and collaboration when they consider each other's perspective in a balanced fashion. Peers also serve as highly available and active companions, providing each other with motivation, imagination, and opportunities for creative elaboration of the activities of their community.[84]

The practice of the cups, as described earlier in the vignette, encapsulates the power of peer learning in Tonya's classroom. In practical terms, this pedagogical move helps Tonya; it serves as a visual reminder that enables her to understand where her students are in their process and where she might need to direct additional support. But it also communicates to students that sharing their process is important, not something to be embarrassed by or to hide away. When students declare with their red cups that they are stuck, the question Tonya asks them in response—"Did you ask your neighbor?"—reminds them that one of the best ways to learn and progress is to interact with those around them, to talk through what they are thinking about and trying to do. Sharing your struggles is a way to help yourself make progress and, through collaborative effort, a way to help others make progress, reflecting Rogoff's observation that thinking is not a "solitary endeavor."[85] And as Rogoff explained, there is something special in the contribution that peers can make to our understanding, because we don't consider their perspective to be determining. We see them as like ourselves, which potentially makes us more open to working with their ideas in ways that don't subsume our own.

Rogoff also recognized that even those with greater expertise are themselves learners within the learning situation. As she described,

> The expert is relatively more skilled than the novices, with a broader vision of the important features of the culturally valued activity. However, the expert too is still developing breadth and depth of skill and understanding in the process of carrying out the activity and guiding others in it.[86]

We can see this duality—teacher as guide, teacher as learner—at play in Tonya's classroom. Tonya is skilled at structuring guidance, employing strategies like the cups and knowing which students to connect to each other. But she also embraces her own evolving expertise. For example, Tonya described her own difficulties with a video game design unit that the students do, remarking:

> I can't even make it past the first level of their games. I can't. So when they ask me for help I just kind of laugh, like, "You're asking me? Ask that kid over there." I'm okay with that. I'm still working on finishing my quest three years later.

When Tonya shares with her students that she doesn't know something, the warmth and humor with which she asserts it reinforce that her words are genuine, not a performance. For Tonya, this kind of interaction is not just about lessening students' dependence on her in an abstract way, it is connected specifically to what she values in learning, to the kinds of thinking and experiences she wants to open up for her students. Conscious of the potential internalized (and externalized) pressure or expectation for a teacher to be all-knowing, she told us:

> I really would challenge teachers to just let go of that concept that you have to know, you have to have all the answers, or you have to be the person that they come to for help. And I think that once teachers can do that, it will allow them to create a space for students to be more creative.

The community that Tonya is creating for her students, the context in which they are engaging in shared problem-solving, is one that embraces moments of not knowing, that celebrates the process of figuring things out, that values what learners have to contribute to one another. If, as Barbara Rogoff helps us see, thinking is not an abstract activity, if it is grounded in our wants and needs, in our interactions with others, then these values themselves are part of what Tonya's students are learning, values that will inform their own individual development and their learning community's collective capacity for creation.

WOULD YOU LIKE TO DO THAT?

Jess's fourth-grade computer students have been designing and coding digital animations, picking topics and themes based on their own interests. After her students have spent some time working and have created initial drafts of their animations, Jess introduces some structures for sharing and feedback. Students take time during class to look at one another's projects, and then respond to the work using a feedback form. The form invites the respondent to share their thoughts on something they liked about the project and something they think could be improved. Students leave thoughtful, specific comments for one another. They say they liked the music, or the way a sprite bounced around. They suggest adding more sounds or more sprites, trying a different background, adding a reset button.

In the next class, students begin by reading the feedback they have received and thinking about it. Jess moves from student to student, asking them to tell her about the feedback they received, listening as they read each comment aloud and reflecting on what it means. Jess then asks the creators, "Would you like to do that? Do you want to act on those suggestions?" She reminds them that feedback is not obligatory; it is an important resource to help them create something meaningful and successful.

One student who has made a game about squirrels agrees with his peers' reactions that the game was too hard, and sets about trying to make it more accessible. Another student explains that the noises others found distracting weren't intentional, and decides to rerecord the sound for his animation so that it is clearer. Another states firmly that she doesn't agree with the comments that more sounds are needed in her animation—she likes it the way it is.

In one corner of the room, Jess listens as a student reads their feedback. The comments reflect that others appreciated how the creator used their own voice for the characters but had some suggestions to improve the background of the animation. Jess asks her, "Do you want to improve the background?" The student responds, "Well, I could change it to the ocean." A classmate sitting nearby remarks, "That's what I was thinking when I suggested that. You could also have more characters if it's going to be a party." As students work toward the final version of their projects, many include acknowledgments thanking others for their comments and help.

When we spoke with Jess about the design of this project, she shared that she had been recently inspired by a book about critical responses to artistic work.[87] The book underscored how creative work benefits from the perspective of others when the feedback process is well structured, respecting both the creator and those offering ideas about the work. With this assignment, Jess wanted her students to understand that creation isn't an entirely individualized process. But she also wanted her students to understand that they still had choice and autonomy in their interactions with others. She wanted them to learn to choose how and when they might engage with feedback. This way of thinking about peer feedback was informed by Jess's broader aspirations for learners in the classroom, including a firmly articulated commitment to supporting students' expressions of autonomy, their ideas about what is important for their learning and why. As she said:

> In my classroom I aim for self-empowerment for both my students and myself. To do this, I aim to provide authentic learning experiences that involve plenty of choice. I want students to tap into their interests and passions thereby keeping them self-motivated and responsible for their own learning.

The language that she used in the questions that guided her interactions with students throughout this particular project—"Would you like to do that?" "Do you want to act on those suggestions?"—communicated to students that they are the ones deciding what to do, that the work is by them and for them.

We see the work that Jess is doing with her students here as establishing the foundation for their intrinsic motivation to participate in peer feedback processes, such that it is something they would choose for themselves in the future, for their own reasons and needs. American psychologists and researchers Richard Ryan and Edward Deci, in a 2000 journal article entitled "Self-Determination Theory and the Facilitation of Intrinsic Motivation, Social Development, and Well-Being," described how intrinsic motivation serves as the foundation for learning and creativity, central to the human drive to explore and develop. As they wrote:

> The fullest representations of humanity show people to be curious, vital, and self-motivated. At their best, they are agentic and inspired, striving to learn; extend themselves, master new skills; and apply their talents responsibly.[88]

Ryan and Deci demonstrated that when people engaged in activities for their own reasons, because they wanted to and found the activity meaningful, their engagement was deeper, what they took from the activity was more lasting, and they were simply happier doing it. So often as teachers we know that peer feedback is valuable for learning and creation, yet we struggle with how to make it feel meaningful rather than obligatory, not just one more thing we are asking students to do. The specific way Jess invites her students into peer feedback, through the central message that it is their decision what to take up, or not, as suits their purposes, gives them space to come to that sense of meaning and value on their own.

In their research, Ryan and Deci explored the nature of environments that either facilitated or undermined the development and expression of intrinsic motivation. The authors offered that environments conducive to intrinsic motivation were ones that addressed three core "psychological needs" whose presence was of central importance to human flourishing in ways that had not previously been recognized. First, they argued that for people to experience intrinsic motivation they needed to have a sense of *autonomy*, which we have seen as central to Jess's classroom practices. In the project in general and in peer feedback specifically, students are given substantive choices about the work they do and how to do it. Jess addresses them as agentic beings, communicating to them that they are the ones who ultimately decide what to do.

Second, Ryan and Deci called out the need to experience *competence*. Students would not be motivated to take up peer feedback practices if they did not see how those practices actually contributed to their own learning, to the improvement of their work. Jess facilitates this experience by asking them questions and connecting them to resources that help them better understand how to actually accomplish what they have decided to do, such that the feedback contributes to their ability to enact their own visions.

And finally, Ryan and Deci observed that situations in which people were able to develop and exercise intrinsic motivation were often characterized by a sense of *relatedness*, of connection with and care from others. They argued that all three of these core psychological needs must be satisfied, that it was detrimental for one to come at the expense of another. For example, people won't experience intrinsic motivation for an activity if they are able to exercise autonomy but without the necessary supports to achieve competence in what they are doing. It is a frequent misconception that the expression of autonomy—being fully yourself, being motivated by your own ideas of what you should do and what is important—means being disconnected from others. Referring to the idea of volition, of learners exercising their own intention and will in what they do, Ryan and Deci wrote, "Autonomy refers not to being independent, detached, or selfish but rather to the feeling of volition that can accompany any act, whether dependent or independent, collectivist or individualist."[89]

One of the most striking features of Jess's classroom is the way in which she communicates to learners a commitment to their expression of autonomy and a commitment to their connection with, support of, and responsibility toward one another. She demonstrates that needs for autonomy and relatedness are mutually supportive, rather than in tension. Even as she tells them that feedback is not obligatory, she adds, "If you start seeing a pattern, like if two people commented on the sound, well then, that would be worth looking at, or interesting to be aware of." Jess communicates to her students that they must give feedback seriously, and take feedback seriously, but that seriousness does not mean they have to do what someone else suggests, or that they expect someone else will necessarily do what they suggest. Instead, it is their sense of volition that is important, that they are taking up or declining to take up these suggestions, as motivated by their own sense of purpose in their work, their own vision for their project. In the classroom as design studio, following your own judgment and vision does not mean isolation from others, and drawing on support from others doesn't mean a lack of autonomy and agency.

CAN YOU TEACH THAT TO ME?

Mary, a fifth-grade science and social studies teacher, has been teaching for over forty years. After learning about a new visual programming language in an online community for teachers, Mary introduces it to her students. She's excited about the potential for them to synthesize and express their content learning in a different medium. She's also excited for them to have an opportunity to develop understandings of coding and computer science, which she believes all learners should have. As she encourages them to explore this new programming language, Mary shares her own developing knowledge and emerging technical competency, saying to her students, "I can do a little bit but not that much yet."

On a warm day in June, the fifth graders use the programming language to create digital animations illustrating changing states of matter. Mary moves about the room but doesn't intervene much in the students' projects. Students are comfortable working together and rarely ask her for help, instead pointing to each other's screens and helping one another figure out how to make things happen. One student leans over a computer screen to show her partner something, who then replies with disbelief, "Wait, you can do that?" Two students are drawing a beaker in the image editor. As Mary passes by, she remarks, "I have a hard time doing that." Another student explains to a visitor to the classroom that day how he figured out how to animate particles moving and bouncing off walls. A pair of learners sits together at a table, lost in thought, not talking, before finally turning to one another and deciding that their animation will be structured around a talk show host presenting the different states of matter.

Sometimes, though, it can be more of a struggle for students to feel comfortable in the learning space Mary has created for them. One student has been socially isolated and disengaged from the classroom work since the beginning of the year. But the introduction of the new programming language piques his interest. He moves through a progressive series of coding challenges Mary has provided, creating impressive project after impressive project. Finally, after he completes an especially difficult project, Mary and the other students in the classroom celebrate him, loudly and enthusiastically, clapping and cheering in support of what he's accomplished.

His interest in coding is ignited by this experience, and Mary supports him in pursuing that interest beyond what the rest of the class is working on, and beyond her own knowledge of programming. She finds him books that help him learn the fundamentals of web development. The student proudly shows Mary the different projects he has been creating on his own time. In response, Mary smiles, saying, "Can you teach that to me?"

When Mary spoke with us about her aspirations for her students, she drew on her own experiences in school. She described herself as a student who wasn't confident in herself, who didn't speak up. She ascribed this to the culture of learning that dominated when she was in school, one in which "teachers had more power. We were a little bit more afraid of them. We couldn't really come up with our own ideas that much." Mary wants something different for her students, for them to have "confidence in their ideas," for them to know "that their idea is just as good as others'." This goal informs both Mary's style as a teacher in the classroom and how she hopes students will engage with their learning experiences. As she explained:

> Mostly I am a facilitator, a guide. I don't try to tell them the answers even when I know them. I'll say, "I don't know. Look that up or go ask Jimmy over there." I try not to give them the answers. Yes, I can probably give you the answer—but that's not getting you to think. It's making me think and putting my ideas onto you. I need you to think. I rarely would just say, "Here's the answer." Even if it was a math question. Because it's easy for the kid to accept that this must be the right answer, because that's what the teacher said.

The actions we see Mary taking here seek to help her students develop confidence in their own ideas, and restructure the learning situation so that it is not about trying to produce answers that they think she knows or has. She introduces them to a new programming language and encourages them to explore when their knowledge outpaces her own. She doesn't intervene as students work to figure things out on their own in their digital animations, communicating to them that they will be able to do it. She celebrates a student in need of support and then enables him to pursue a topic of interest on his own, asking him to teach her what he can do.

In their 1969 book *Teaching as a Subversive Activity*, American educators Neil Postman and Charles Weingartner argued that learners having confidence in their own ideas, in their own thinking, should be the purpose of education. Postman and Weingartner were reacting to the same kinds of educational experiences that Mary described herself having, in which education was about control, about the imposition of ideas onto students. The authors were concerned with the thriving of a democratic society, which they asserted was only possible through its members thinking and acting for themselves.

But they were also concerned with thriving on the individual, human level, with how opportunities for genuine intellectual exploration are intertwined with experiences of joy and human connection. We see this attention to human thriving in the work of Mary and other teachers in the classroom as design studio, as the aspirations that inform their pedagogical actions go beyond any specific assignment, subject, or year, and cannot be captured by narrow concepts such as "college and career readiness" that so frequently dominate conversations about K–12 education. These are aspirations about the kind of people they hope the young learners in their classrooms will be, a hope for them to engage with the world within and beyond the classroom with interest and confidence, believing in themselves as people with something to say, confident that they can figure things out, and excited to encounter new ideas as they go.

Postman and Weingartner described themselves as "simple, romantic men"[90] in relation to school. They believed, centrally and profoundly, that school can make things better, that school can be the mechanism through which young people discover that they can learn how to think for themselves and learn why thinking for themselves is so important. And the authors emphasized that the core means by which learners develop this confidence in their ideas is the work of their teacher. It is significant that they titled a book about their hopes for students *Teaching as a Subversive Activity*. They asserted that it is teachers' beliefs about learners and learning that inform how teachers structure the classroom, design activities, and interact with their students, and thus inform what messages students receive about themselves from those interactions and work. As the authors wrote:

> Let us consider here the teachers, and especially their *attitudes*. We take it as axiomatic that the attitudes of teachers are the most important characteristic of the inquiry environment. This point is frequently passed over even by those who advocate the use of inquiry methods, but especially by those innovators who are in constant quest of "teacher-proof" programs and methodologies. *There can be no significant innovation in education that does not have at its center the attitudes of teachers, and it is an illusion to think otherwise.* The beliefs, feelings, and assumptions of teachers are the air of a learning environment; they determine the quality of life within it.[91]

As Mary cautioned, just as a teacher can communicate to their students that teachers hold all the knowledge and are the arbiters of right and wrong, a teacher can also communicate to students that the students themselves have ideas of value, worthy of expression and recognition. Mary's actions as a teacher are grounded in her belief in her students' capabilities as human beings, and her desire for them to believe in themselves in ways that further future learning. This belief is the air of her classroom environment, it pervades and surrounds all the work that is going on. It is communicated in the nature of her decisions about when to intervene or not, and the form that intervention takes.

Postman and Weingartner also noted that sharing in an aspiration to help learners have confidence in their own ideas doesn't prescribe a single method of teaching or a specific set of curricular materials. As teachers in the classroom as design studio, we all have different styles and approaches—some more structured, some more traditionally academic, some more constrained by curriculum and testing. But it is this shared aspiration—a belief in all learners as people with ideas who can act upon the world, figure things out for themselves, and make things of meaning and value—that unites us, and thus, we hope, enriches the experiences of our students.

YOU'VE GOT THIS, RIGHT?

When visitors or administrators walk into Leslie's middle school technology classroom, it often takes them a moment to locate her. Students are spread throughout the room, working on computer programs, as Leslie remains purposefully on the periphery, walking around the room and watching students work. Today, Leslie passes by one student who is working intently on her program. Leslie admires the work and remarks, "Wow! You've got this, right?" The student nods in confirmation and Leslie moves on.

Nearby, she hears a student, who has been working quietly, blurt out in frustration, "I can't get it!" Leslie moves over to the student, standing next to him, and responds, with quiet conviction, "Yes, you can." She moves away, but keeps an eye on the student from across the room. Leslie watches for a few minutes as the student sits lost in thought and then, finally, begins to try something else.

During another day's class, one student remarks with disdain that she hates algebra. Leslie reminds her that she recently figured out how to use variables in her coding project, and adds, "You were pretty great at it." In a quiet moment, she remarks to a student, "You're good at this. You might want to consider doing more with it." To another student she shares, "You could probably teach me something right now!" When a student is reluctant to share his work with the class, Leslie respects his choice. Wanting to acknowledge the excellence of the student's project as well as his efforts, she tells him privately, "This is the best work you've ever done."

Leslie has a profound belief in the capabilities of her middle school students—and we see this belief reflected in her pedagogical moves. By asking, "You've got this, right?," by telling students they can do it, that they're good at this, that they can teach her something, Leslie is making a purposeful choice to lend the authority of her position as teacher to her validation of students' own capacities to act and succeed independently of her. When Leslie is holding back from intervening, prompting her students to figure out something on their own or to seek out a peer for help, she is doing it so that they will have the opportunity to exercise and recognize their own capacity, rather than feeling dependent on her. And when she does step in—to encourage someone, to name specifically something they are doing well—she does so in ways that convey the same fundamental belief in students' capacity and support their own recognition of that capacity. Leslie wants her students to share her belief in them.

When Leslie explained to us why it was important to her to make space for students to engage in open-ended coding projects where they could figure things out and express their own ideas, she emphasized the connection between such work and students' belief in themselves: "I like to have students figure out that they're good at things that they might not know that they're good at. I like how it brings out skills that kids didn't know that they had." Leslie went on to connect her practice of calling students' attention to their strengths and accomplishments to her concerns about the lack of women and people of color in computer science, and her knowledge that such representation could be impacted by these individuals' early experiences in school and the extent to which those experiences supported or undermined their confidence that they could do advanced work in the field.

This conviction is a cornerstone of American educational researcher Gloria Ladson-Billings's theory of culturally relevant pedagogy, along with its grounding in a sense of the reciprocity between students' experiences in the classroom and broader structural inequalities in society. As documented in her prolific writing, including her 1995 article "Toward a Theory of Culturally Relevant Pedagogy" and her 2021 essay collection *Culturally Relevant Pedagogy: Asking a Different Question*, Ladson-Billings's work was originally motivated by her concerns with the prevalence of deficit models as a way of talking about Black students and their educational needs. As she argued, when schools and teachers see themselves as superior to parents and communities and fail to work with them, fail to recognize the strengths that all learners bring to the classroom, and fail to see the specificity of learners' lived experiences as assets to draw upon, they cannot help all learners to thrive and grow.

Ladson-Billings's research focused on teachers who created classroom cultures in which Black learners were successful, but her findings about these teachers' beliefs and actions can inform teaching practices that enable many different types of learners to engage and grow in the classroom. Two of her findings are especially resonant with characteristics of the classroom as design studio. First, she found that these teachers believed deeply that all students were capable of rich intellectual work, and that they communicated this belief directly to students. Observing that "the teachers in my study focused on the strengths and assets students brought to the learning environment,"[92] she described teachers sharing with their students many different versions of Leslie's "You've got this, right?" affirmation—both explicitly and implicitly through the work they were invited into and their encouragement that students continue to engage in that work even when it was difficult.

Second, Ladson-Billings found that these teachers' classrooms were characterized by forms of social relations that differed from those traditionally found in classrooms. As she described:

> In these teachers' classrooms, the teacher-student relationships are equitable and reciprocal. All of the teachers gave students opportunities to act as teachers. In one class, the teacher regularly sat at a student's desk while the student stood at the front of the room and explained a concept or some aspect of student culture. Another teacher highlighted the expertise of students and required other students to consult those students before coming to her for help: "Did you ask Jamal how to do those math problems?" "Make sure you check with Latasha before you turn in your reading."[93]

These social relations are part of what communicates to learners a belief in their capacity. When Leslie tells a student that they could teach *her* something, it contributes to that belief. And, as Ladson-Billings asserted, both of these qualities are enabled by a sense of connectedness between teachers and students, which we see in Leslie's classroom as she checks in with student after student, making sure they have what they need, reassuring them they can do the work, and validating what they've done. But, as Ladson-Billings cautioned, it is entirely inadequate to just tell students that they are doing well, absent substantive and grounded experiences of learning. When Leslie tells a student, "Yes, you can," and then walks away, she keeps observing, ready to provide the supports or intervention necessary to enable the student to engage with the work meaningfully.

Many elements of the classroom as design studio—the use of open-ended projects, the greater space for learners to pursue their own questions and figure out their own approaches to doing things, the honoring of multiple ways of knowing—have historically been seen as the province of privileged or rarified educational spaces. This sequestering of educational opportunity, and its consequent replication of structural inequality, is grounded in the deficit view of learners that Ladson-Billings called out—either a lack of belief that all learners can do this work, or a belief that other skills need to be remediated before it is even a possibility. For Leslie and other teachers in the classroom as design studio, the fundamental belief organizing their pedagogy is that this work is for everyone.

WHAT ARE YOU TRYING TO DO?

As Melanie, an elementary technology teacher, reviews her materials in preparation for teaching an animated music video programming project again this year, she frowns at the rubric she used last year. It was a conventional rubric, presenting a series of performance categories, each scored from 0 to 4 points, depending on the degree of completion or sophistication of the work. She feels frustrated with how this rubric seemed to focus on what is missing and deficient about student work, rather than recognizing what her students had been able to create, what matters to them, and what they might do next.

Melanie cares deeply about learners and their intentions. As they are making progress on their projects, when students in Melanie's elementary technology classrooms hit stumbling blocks or ask her for help, she typically responds by asking questions like "What are you trying to do?" and "What is your goal?" to better understand what is important to them. She wonders how she can better align her commitment to recognizing her students' intentions and aspirations with how she assesses their work. She wants assessment to celebrate what her students have done, honor their intentions for their projects, and help them look forward.

Melanie decides that this year she will try using a single-point rubric. As with the previous rubric, this style of rubric includes a series of performance categories, such as specific programming features and design elements. But for each category, instead of points, she offers a comment about a current strength and a suggestion for potential growth. She decides to add categories for "self-expression," which reflects her understanding of a student's individual expression through the work, and for "initiative," which explicitly acknowledges a student's perseverance and debugging efforts. She also decides to invite students to revise their work after receiving this feedback and to respond to her notes.

Melanie is excited about this new direction for assessment, which she hopes will honor students' freedom and encourage their developing knowledge.

In our conversations with her, Melanie described her aspirations for the learners in her classroom, aspirations that underlie the questions she asks her students while they are working on their projects. "What I want them to do is to experiment," she said. "I don't want to hand them too much. I want them to figure out things and realize that they can do all of this stuff." But she acknowledged there were external pressures that could sometimes work against these aspirations. For example, to meet the administration's approval, she had to give students a grade, both for specific projects and for the marking period as a whole. She felt a tension between satisfying that administrative expectation and realizing her desire for her students to experiment and explore. As she mused, "How do you really grade creativity?"

Melanie worked to realize her aspirations within these constraints by tinkering with her assessment rubric. The changes she made to her rubric and how she used it with her students reflect a move to assessment as something her students can use for their learning, for their creative process, rather than an external measure that signaled an endpoint to their work. Rather than assigning a number that potentially leaves students feeling that they did something wrong, Melanie provides comments that her students can use to move their work forward, along with an opportunity to revise and then resubmit. She includes categories related to self-expression and initiative to honor learners' creative processes, how they are going about the work and what it might mean to them, and their evolving capabilities with this type of creative work that involves exploration, experimentation, and discovery.

It was precisely these kinds of aspirations—and the constraints of traditional schooling that could work against them—that motivated American psychologist Carl Rogers to write his 1969 book for educators entitled *Freedom to Learn*. His work as a psychologist informed his belief in the fundamental need, drive, and capacity of all people to be self-determining agents who work, over a lifetime, to become the most fully realized versions of themselves, and Rogers saw how education, at all levels, could either painfully constrain or powerfully support this process. He contrasted the rote learning of decontextualized and prescribed material with what he called "significant or experiential learning,"[94] which he described in the following manner:

> I am talking about the student who says, "I am discovering, drawing in from the outside, and making what I discover a real part of *me*." I am talking about any learning in which the experience of the learner progresses along this line: "No, no, that's not what I want."; "Wait! This is closer to what I'm interested in, what I need."; "Ah, here it is! Now I'm grasping and comprehending what I *need* and what I want to know!"[95]

When Melanie describes her aspirations for learners to explore and experiment, when she asks her students what their goals are in moments of struggle or uncertainty, when she works to make assessment something her students can use to advance their learning, she is trying to help her students see themselves as people with ideas, as people who make decisions about their learning.

Throughout the rest of his book, Rogers described a variety of environments where such learning can take place, from a sixth-grade classroom to a graduate seminar in psychology. This variety was purposeful. As Rogers noted, "It seems important to show that such significant, self-initiated, experiential learning is *possible*, that it is possible in sharply different kinds of educational situations, and that it produces self-reliant learners."[96] Through the stories of different classrooms we have assembled in our book, we have endeavored to offer a similar variety, motivated by a similar purpose. Some teachers have more latitude than other teachers to determine their curriculum, to make changes to the structures and routines of classrooms, to adopt alternative forms of assessment. We all do the work of teaching within constraints. The specifics of those constraints can differ, and we might further differ from one another in how much we agree or disagree with the rationale and value of the constraints under which we work. Yet, as Rogers argued, we all want to create learning experiences in which our students can find meaning and satisfaction, can express themselves, and can grow as unique individuals. As such, we continuously strive to adapt our classrooms to make possible these kinds of learning experiences, while working within our specific constraints, as Melanie does.

A focus on meaning, satisfaction, expression, and growth is a defining characteristic of the classroom as design studio and it would not be possible without some element of open-ended work, some space for freedom of choice and expression for students. But focusing too narrowly on the quantity of open-ended work can obscure the importance of the quality of the experience. As Rogers explained:

> Judging by my own experience and that of others, the *amount* of freedom which can be given to the group is not particularly important. The class and the instructor may have to accept the constrictions of a rigid examination, of a pre-set curriculum and text, and other limitations. What is important is that within these limits the freedom that is given is *real*, is not hesitantly or guardedly given by the leader, and is perceived as real by the students. Then—even in a seemingly narrow sector of their work—they can experience freedom of choice, freedom of expression, freedom to be.[97]

So although Melanie's specific assessment adaptations might not be a possibility for every teacher given constraints they need to accept, Melanie's practice of asking students genuine questions about their intentions, such as "What are you trying to do?" can be applied by any teacher. We can ask our students these questions no matter the context: whether they're working on the most open-ended, self-directed projects or solving prescribed problems from a math textbook. Given any classroom constraints, if we ask these questions genuinely and listen sincerely to students' responses, all learners can experience some measure of the freedom that Rogers described: opportunities to be guided by their own goals, judgments, and perspectives.

WHAT DO YOU EXPECT OF YOURSELF?

When Irene was a student in the third grade, her teacher had set up a table at the back of the classroom that was full of curious and playful materials. When they were done with their assigned work, students had the freedom to explore, play, and work on a self-directed project with the materials on the table. As a third grader, Irene often finished early and, reminiscing as an adult, she fondly recalled having the space, time, and materials to work on something under her own direction. Now a high school computer science teacher, Irene returned to these memories when thinking about the types of learning experiences she desired for her students. She wondered: What if every student always had access to that table, to that experience of self-direction, rather than making everything dependent on having completed their teacher-assigned work?

To create this experience in her media design classroom, Irene introduces the *unproject*: a learner-directed experience in which her students decide what to work on, how to work on it, and what it means to them. To launch the unproject experience, Irene co-designs the assessment rubric with her students. The prompt for their rubric design begins with a single question: "What do you expect of yourself?" As students work, Irene uses their articulations of their own goals to support them, reminding them of what they set out to accomplish.

As her students develop their unprojects, Irene sees that some students are struggling with the work. Irene meets with the students who are uncomfortable with the unproject, checking in with them about what they are working on and how they feel about it. For students who seem unenthusiastic about what they are doing, Irene asks them if they are excited about the project, confirming that it is something they definitely want to do. If they aren't excited, Irene works with them to identify a new project that might better fuel their interest and motivation. She regularly reminds students that their own excitement can and should be a driving force in their learning, from the start to the end of the project.

The topics students decide to pursue range widely, reflecting their individual concerns. While the topics and projects are different from ones Irene might choose for them, she is committed to supporting students in pursuing their own goals. One student has always wanted to learn to touch type and designs a ten-session learning sequence for themselves dedicated to this ambition. Another student decides to make a guide for herself and her peers who are starting to look at colleges, providing resources related to choosing schools and navigating financial aid. Yet another student uses a digital illustration tool to draw a powerful image of a woman standing in an ocean, inspired by her own mother, and in doing so reveals artistic passions and commitments that Irene has been unaware of. One of Irene's favorite projects is a collaboration among four students across two classes, some in her Media Design class and some in her AP Computer Science class. They create a game, dividing up the coding and graphic design tasks, and establish organizational systems to help them track and manage the work. They aren't able to finish the game during the in-class time allocated to the project, but they are able to create something they want to keep working on in the future.

When Irene spoke with us about why she designed the unproject and her aspiration to expand it in upcoming years, she referred to her belief that it was important for students to have the chance to determine what they wanted to do but was aware that some students had struggled with those sorts of opportunities when she had presented them in the past. She began to think about why that might be:

> When I do this, who has a hard time? And it seemed to be the students who are a little bit less academically achieving than the others. I started to think why that might be—and it's a theory, I'm working on it. But one of my theories was that they rarely get that opportunity. I remember for good or for bad, I'm kind of like a learner and doer who likes to just be like, "I'm done." And, I remember as a kid feeling really motivated knowing that if I was done, I got to, whatever, write a book report of my choice. You know, a lot of teachers have that built in. And, so have I. So, I thought there are some kids who are almost never getting to the choice project. They're never getting the complete—"What do you want to do?" I wanted to try to get those kids who maybe don't have a chance to set their own goals and I wanted them to have that opportunity.

Irene theorized that, if doing work of one's own design was used as a motivational tool, something to do when you were finished with the assigned work, it remained an experience out of reach of those students who took longer to do their assigned work, those for whom, for a variety of reasons, learning could be more of a struggle, who had fewer experiences of conventional classroom success. Consequently, such learners were stuck in a self-perpetuating cycle, in which they never had the opportunity to practice self-directed work, and thus never had the opportunity to get better at doing it. The unproject is an opportunity to break this cycle. By giving students choice in what to make, by asking them "What do you expect of yourself?" and enabling those expectations to determine the trajectory of their projects, Irene is communicating to her students that they can and should be self-directed.

In the classroom as design studio, the experience of doing a project that the learner has defined, that is important to them for their own purposes, is a fundamental characteristic of the learning experience for all students. In her act of theorizing about the need for these opportunities and the reasons why some students lack them, and by taking steps to create more space for all learners to be self-directed in her classroom, Irene is acting as what Henry Giroux, American-Canadian scholar of education and cultural studies, called a *transformative intellectual*. In his 1988 essay collection *Teachers as Intellectuals: Toward a Critical Pedagogy of Learning*, Giroux wrote that transformative intellectual teachers "are both theoreticians and practitioners, who can combine theory, imagination, and techniques."[98] In reflecting on the self-perpetuating cycle of access to opportunities for self-direction that Irene has identified, she noted that most teachers, herself included, had positive experiences, or were successful, in school. To have your self, your ways of learning and being, validated by the structures of schooling is itself a form of privilege. As Henry Giroux argued, the work of the teacher as transformative intellectual involves engaging in serious critique of one's current context and actions, while creating space for new possibilities and change. This work might begin, Giroux offered, with teachers (and others in the supportive surround with which young people engage) questioning their own experiences and privilege, rather than allowing those experiences to unreflectively impact the learning experiences they structure for students.

But, Giroux argued, the space for reflection must also be accompanied by the space for teachers themselves to experience agency and self-determination, coming to their own conclusions about what is important for student learning, designing curriculum around those conclusions, and iterating on it over time, as we see Irene doing throughout this vignette. This is part of what it means for teachers to act as, to be seen as, intellectuals. Giroux cautioned against the conceptualization of the teacher as mere technician, manifested through the types of materials made available to teachers, a concern he articulated in the late 1980s that is still unfortunately applicable today.

> This becomes evident in many of the "teacher proof" instructional materials now flooding the market. These materials promote a deskilling of teachers by separating conception from execution and by reducing the role that teachers play in the actual creation and teaching of such materials. Teacher decisions about what should be taught, how it might meet the intellectual and cultural needs of students, and how it might be evaluated are rendered unimportant in these packages, since they have already predefined and answered such questions. The materials control teachers' decisions, and, as a result, teachers do not need to exercise reasoned judgment. Thus, teachers are reduced to the role of obedient technicians, carrying out the dictates of the curriculum package.[99]

For teachers to enable the kinds of learning characterized by the classroom as design studio, they must themselves get to choose, act, and decide, informed by their own sense of what is important.

For Irene, her conviction that all learners should have this experience of defining their own project is grounded both in her own experiences and in her sense of what people need in order to be happy and successful in life. Noting that college involves consequential choice (of courses, of paper topics), and that simple everyday acts such as cleaning your house necessitate determining goals, making a plan, and evaluating its success, she expressed her ultimate aspiration for learners in her classroom: "I hope they gain the skills to be able to execute things that they want to do. And, for me, those things don't even have to be necessarily related to the field that I'm teaching, but just sort of that idea of, 'I have a concept and the confidence to work toward executing whatever that is.'"

In this vignette, we see Irene take her aspiration and turn it into meaningful action. She designs the unproject, inviting all learners to define something that is important to them, something they want to spend their time doing. She helps them make a productive plan for work by articulating their own goals and defining what they think success looks like, helping them develop a vision of what they are working toward. When they falter in execution, losing interest or focus, she reminds them to reflect on what they really want, what really excites them in their learning, and let that guide their work. And she celebrates the variety and individuality of their work. In creating these tangible, accessible opportunities for all students to determine their own purposes and exercise meaningful choice, to act as self-directed agents, she is responding to Henry Giroux's call for the transformative potential of public schools. What theorizing and critique enable is acting to make things better. As Giroux wrote:

> Public schools need to be organized around a vision that celebrates not what is but what could be, a vision that looks beyond the immediate to the future, and a vision that links struggle to a new set of human possibilities.[100]

WHAT DOES THIS MEAN TO YOU?

High school computer science teacher Rose feels that the AP curriculum she is using lacks opportunities for open-ended creative work that more accurately mirrors the professional world. Looking to expand her students' experiences, Rose arranges for them to participate in a local industry-sponsored hackathon. Organized in teams of four, the students work over two days to design and build a program, prompted only by the word *community*. Each team is developing a program they care about, seeking out technical knowledge from available mentors as needed. The atmosphere is abuzz with concentration and energy, as students move between silently coding and communicating with group members to plan and problem-solve.

The students create many beautiful projects; through these projects, Rose sees her students connecting to their interests, refining existing coding competence, and exploring computing concepts that are well beyond the high school AP curriculum. One team creates a chat room designed to bring different groups of people together. Another team makes a mobile app to connect people experiencing homelessness to social services and other resources.

One of Rose's favorite projects is from a group of four young women of color. They've created an app called Curl Check, which offers information about products for people with curly or textured hair and connects users to local Black-owned businesses carrying those products. After she hears their description of their app, Rose asks the team, "What does this mean to you?" One team member chimes in, describing the relationship of their app to the broader hackathon theme of community. "This app can bring together people with hair types that aren't seen normally in society. So this app can help people feel like they're being included. It could help the whole natural hair community come closer together and support each other more than they could've before."

Rose observes how powerful it is for the students to have made something that was meaningful to them and to have had the opportunity to see themselves, as creators and designers, in the office of a large, influential technology company. As one student shared as she reflected on her favorite part of the experience, "I liked being in this atmosphere. It was cool to see how everything works and be around all the people that were here." The group is invited back by the industry sponsor to present their idea to a group of software engineers. Inspired by their participation in the hackathon, all four students decide to take more courses in computer science, and express an interest in further developing their app.

In our conversations together, Rose shared that the hackathon was "one of the best things I've ever done as a teacher." When asked why, she highlighted several different aspects of the learning experience as being powerful. First, she noted how the open-endedness of the task—offering students just one word and sending them off to figure out what to create, how to do it, and how to work together to achieve their goals—was a rich opportunity for intellectual exploration. She described their engagement, motivation, and excitement, emphasizing the uniqueness of high school students sitting for four hours at a stretch, completely absorbed in their work and focused on their creation. She wondered aloud playfully, "Is that normal?" She saw how invested students were, which enabled them to persist when confronted by technical challenges, to seek out information about how to do things they didn't know yet, all in the service of turning their visions into reality.

But she also spoke about the value of the experience in terms of her students' ideas about themselves, and their relationship to computer science. For her, the hackathon represented an opportunity for her students to see themselves as belonging to this professional culture of computing. As she explained,

> Ultimately I want students to think that computer science is a career that they can pursue, that there's a lot more in it than what is stereotypically thought of. And so providing students with creativity and creative projects and allowing

them to investigate their own interests allows them to see themselves in computer science.

Through the design of this learning experience, Rose is engaging with the cultural understanding of computer science, what it means to do the work of computer science, and who gets to claim the identity of a computer scientist.

Rose is attuned to what Jamaican-born English cultural theorist Stuart Hall helps us understand as the hegemonic, or dominant, views of the computer science field—as white and male, as narrowly technical and abstract. In work such as his 1973 essay "Encoding/Decoding," Hall called attention to language and culture as a site in which power plays out. As he wrote:

> The definition of a hegemonic viewpoint is (a) that it defines within its terms the mental horizon, the universe, of possible meanings, of a whole sector of relations in a society or culture; and (b) that it carries with it the stamp of legitimacy—it appears coterminous with what is "natural," "inevitable," "taken for granted" about the social order.[101]

Rose wants to challenge the dominant cultural associations her students may have of computer science, and with those associations their own ideas about what they might be capable of. She does not want it to seem inevitable that computer science is embodied in the "white, male, nerd stereotype" that she describes as prevalent in high school computer science. Rose sees the open-ended, self-directed creation of the hackathon experience as central to her students seeing, feeling, and believing in themselves as capable of doing the work of software designers and engineers. It is a combination of how they understand the work and how they understand themselves. When the work allows for creation, they can find themselves in it, and when they can find themselves in it, this engagement can support an evolving sense of their own capacity. She saw the impact of this on the young women who created the Curl Check app, in their continuing on in their computer science learning, their desire to do more with their creation, and their sense of belonging in a professional environment that might previously have seemed out of reach, as the domain of others.

Offering this different meaning of computer science—what it is and who gets to do it—is something Rose is doing intentionally. But, as Stuart Hall reminds us, meaning is made at the intersection of what is offered and what is received. Hall presented a profoundly different way of thinking about communication, challenging the behaviorist assumptions of much research that focused on how to "make" people take from a message or experience what was intended by those who created it. As he wrote, "There is no necessary correspondence between encoding and decoding—the former can attempt to 'pre-fer' but cannot prescribe or guarantee the latter, which has its own conditions of existence."[102]

We can't, ultimately, control the meaning that someone else makes of a word, or an experience—how they, in Hall's words, decode it. The "conditions of existence" Hall referred to have everything to do with who people are as individuals, with the experiences, social positioning, beliefs, and personalities that they bring to an exchange or interaction. Rose wanted her students to engage with these dominant ideas about computer science but, as shown by the language in which these young women describe the significance of their design, they were already thinking about power, culture, and society, about visibility and invisibility, about who does and doesn't get to speak for what is needed and important.

The meaning that these students made in their project was something only they could determine. What this group chose to do with the opportunity afforded by the hackathon was about who they were as individuals, about their own identities and experiences as young women of color, what they valued and what they wanted to create in response. Rose did not choose, and could not have chosen, this project for them. But she created the "conditions of existence"—through a learning experience in which these ideas were possible to have and to make real. Rose valued the open-endedness of the hackathon task, and other creative projects she designed in her classroom, precisely because they left space for learners' own ideas, space for them to make their own meaning, rather than presenting that meaning as foreclosed or overly determined. Rose asks her students, "What does this mean to you?" because she does not specifically know. It is their meaning, not hers.

WHAT DOES QUALITY MEAN TO YOU?

The middle school students in Penny's computer science classroom will be designing and coding digital math games to help elementary students who are working on their developing number sense and fact fluency. Penny frames the project as an opportunity to help others, and encourages the middle schoolers to reflect on their own experiences in elementary school. She invites her students' ideas about what the project could be and encourages them to explore different paths. As they start their projects, students are making decisions about the level of difficulty they want their games to have and the areas of math they want to focus on. One student comes up to Penny and says, "I was reading a lot more about number sense. Instead of making a game, could I talk about number sense and put some things in that maybe a parent would look at to be able to help their child?" Penny responds, "Oh, absolutely. That would be fantastic!"

As students develop their projects, Penny asks them to think about the question "What does quality mean to you?" The class works collaboratively to co-design a rubric that identifies components of a quality project. Drawing on their understanding of the needs and experiences of the elementary students for whom they are designing, Penny's students articulate multiple dimensions they want to include in the rubric. One student focuses on accuracy in support of learning, offering, "Well, the math should be correct. If we're testing them on multiplication, then our answers have to be correct." Another student raises the importance of the aesthetic dimensions of a game and its impact on engagement, suggesting, "There should be some kind of color. It should be good to look at." A third considers professionalism and presentation, noting, "There shouldn't be any grammar or spelling errors."

Using the qualities the students have identified, Penny creates the five-point rubric she will use for grading—and only the games assessed as the highest quality will be shared with the elementary school students. After an initial round of assessment with the rubric, not all the games the middle schoolers have created initially meet the standard. While revisions are not a required part of the assignment, the middle schoolers are excited to continue working until they have made something worthy of the younger learners for whom they are creating, saying to her, "I want to do more" and "I want my program to be good enough to go to the elementary schools." One student seeks Penny's help, saying that they want to improve their project, and asking her, "What can I do?"

In this project, we see how Penny's students have a profound sense of ownership over their work. She's designed the conditions to foster this sense of ownership in this assignment, inviting students to choose their own project topics, exploring their own understanding of what it means to help elementary students learn math. When Penny explained why it was important to her to create the conditions in which this sense of ownership could flourish, she drew on her own fraught experiences in school.

> One reason I hated school is because I don't like being told, "This is what you have to do." As soon as someone tells me that this is what I have to do—and this is really the child in me still as an adult—then I still just don't want to do it. So, when I have a bunch of students, the idea that I'm going to come up with something that's going to grab all of them is not really a viable thought, so I always tell them, "I am open to negotiation." I like to respect when someone else, when a student comes up to me and says, "I have a different take on this."

Penny's commitment to respecting students' own ideas—and the sense of ownership over their work that results—extends not only to what students are making, but also to their assessment of what they've made, to what quality means to them. Her students have ideas about what will make their projects worthwhile and meaningful; they establish criteria for quality and work hard to ensure their own work meets those standards. Penny is required by her school to give grades to all student projects, even though she has reservations about doing so. But she draws on the students' ideas of quality to determine the rubric that she uses to grade the assignments.

Penny observed how this participation in generating the assessment for the project promoted students' sense of ownership over what they were making. They decide what their success looks like, instead of their teacher telling them what their success is going to look like. That she supported the criteria the students generated—their focus on accuracy, engagement, and professionalism—was further evidence of her commitment to respecting and trusting their ideas for their work. Penny starts from a place of trust: "I think the best thing to do is to see each student as wanting to produce quality."

In her 1983 book *Lessons from a Child: On the Teaching and Learning of Writing*, American writing teacher and researcher Lucy Calkins told a similar story of the power of ownership. Drawing on her extensive ethnographic research, Calkins described the transformation of a group of third graders who went from seeing writing as something they were told to do to seeing writing as something they wanted and needed to do for their own reasons. While this transformation began simply, with students choosing the topics on which they wrote, it became central to their relationship to revision. The students were developing ideas about what made writing—their own writing, the writing of others—good or not, and how to make it better. In articulating the importance of these ideas, Calkins referenced thoughts shared by developmental psychologist and fellow researcher of learning Howard Gardner upon observing the classrooms included in Calkins's study and one of the participants, a girl named Susie. As Calkins recounted:

> Researchers from Canada, Australia and Great Britain as well as the United States have visited our research site and studied our data. They've all had questions—many questions—but it was Howard Gardner who asked the simplest, most difficult question of all: "What is Susie trying to do when she writes?" he asked. "What are her goals, her concepts of good writing?" . . . Gardner's question has been omnipresent, for Susie's intentions were at the root of her activities. Because her writing involved an interplay of creation and criticism, her writing was propelled by concern for meaning making . . . and it was guided and shaped by concepts of good writing. Susie built and rebuilt her sense of good while she operated within it.[103]

As with Penny's students, the young writers in Susie's classroom had their own goals and purposes for their work. Implicated in this sense of ownership were their own ideas about what quality meant to them. These ideas gave substance to their taking up of processes of revision, to sharing work with one another and looking for ways to improve it.

Calkins called attention to two mechanisms through which the young writers she studied were able to develop these ideas about quality as part of their writing process, both of which we see present in Penny's classroom: creating opportunities to interact with an audience and decentering the teacher's perspective. The first mechanism is the power of making something for an audience. Calkins observed how Susie finds her voice by writing for the peers in her classroom, motivated by a desire to simultaneously entertain them as readers and help them understand her own experiences. For Penny's students, creating games for the audience of elementary students learning math gives the middle schoolers both motivation for producing work they consider to be of quality but also specific ideas for what quality looks like in that context. Making something *for* someone gives weight and meaning to the process of creation; you want to make something worthwhile to the person you're creating for. As Penny shared with us, it wasn't that the students were thinking, "I want an A." It was that they wanted their games to be good enough for the elementary students. They went above and beyond the requirements because they were responding to the needs of their audience. Calkins helps us see that this responsiveness to a real audience is part of learners developing their own ideas of what is important in their work. She described the third graders asking each other the kinds of questions that their teachers were asking them about their writing—"How did it feel?" "What are you going to do next?"—and then starting to ask themselves these questions, without anyone else present, a process one of the students referred to as a "conference with yourself."[104]

Focusing on audience also means a move away from the teacher as primary recipient and judge of student work, which is the second mechanism Calkins recognized. Greater student ownership is enabled by the teacher inhabiting a different role in the classroom, taking the students, their work, and their ideas about their work seriously. Not only does Penny respect students' ideas for what they want their projects to be, but she asks them what they think a quality project looks like. Rather than telling them her ideas, Penny incorporates her students' criteria into the rubric used for actual grading. Calkins noted how, in our desire to help learners, we can often do them harm through rushing in with our ideas of how to make their work better, reinforcing the sense that they are dependent on us to know what is of value, and dismissing the ideas that they themselves bring. Describing her role as a teacher in a student conference, a one-on-one meeting with a student to discuss their work, Calkins wrote about how that power imbalance can manifest itself.

As teachers, we've all done our share of perpetuating children's dependence on our ideas. I, too, have approached a conference thinking, "What would I do if this draft were mine? How would I improve on it?" Somehow it's so much easier to write someone else's piece than to write my own! Sometimes I've quite literally taken the writing out of the writer's hands and held it in my own: what a message. Taking control has also come in the form of my speaking first. I assume the writer has nothing to say, that he or she is a blank slate waiting for my wisdom, and so I impose my agenda onto the conference. Specific questions, meant to coax writers to expand my favorite sections, are another way of taking over a child's draft. "What colors were the flowers?" I ask, implying that this information belongs in the draft. But who is to say if the color of the flowers was important to the writer?[105]

Calkins wrote admiringly of teachers, like Penny, whose conferences with students gave students the space to articulate what they thought of their work. That space offers students the power to develop their own sense of themselves as learners and a sense of ownership over their work. To respect learners' own ideas for what quality means to them is to respect their ideas for what is important to them. This is the work of teaching in the classroom as design studio, supporting students in becoming self-determining and responsible in their own learning, helping them develop trust in their own perspectives on what is important and why.

WHAT WOULD YOU LIKE TO SHOWCASE?

Toward the end of a class session in the middle of the school year, veteran middle school computing teacher Kristine finds herself with some extra time before the bell signaling the end of the day. She spontaneously decides to invite students to show something they have been working on. She usually doesn't do this until she thinks the work is in a more finished state, ready in her assessment to be shown off to others. To her surprise, her students respond with enthusiastic exclamations: "Mine! Mine! Show mine!" Everyone in the room seems excited about the opportunity, both those who want to share and those who would serve as audience for the sharing.

A few months later, Kristine starts planning the Family Technology Literacy Night at her school. An annual event, she has typically organized this as a showcase of students' creations, where she decides which projects should be displayed to the attendees. She initially proceeds as she has done in the past, going over the projects her students have completed throughout the year and identifying ones that she thinks should be shared. But Kristine finds her thoughts returning to the class that ended with the unexpected sharing of student work and the enthusiasm students expressed. She can feel herself starting to change her ideas about what a showcase can be and what it is celebrating in student learning.

She sends an email to all of her classes, writing, "We have an opportunity to showcase our work. I want to know, what would you like to showcase? Send me a link or send me the project." Kristine quickly receives many enthusiastic responses, with students eager to share projects they most loved working on throughout the year. When the night of the showcase arrives, students start setting up their projects on the computers in the classroom. In preparation, each student has written a brief description of the project they're sharing, accompanied by a short biography, which Kristine has put in a handmade frame placed next to the student and their computer. Staff, parents, and students from across the school walk around and look at what Kristine's students have created.

Even though Kristine had long held a belief in the importance of creating opportunities for students to explore and create, to make things that felt reflective of them and what they cared about, she hadn't previously questioned her decisions about what work to show and when. She first recognized the potential power of those decisions when she opened up sharing of in-progress work in an unplanned, unexpected moment at the end of class. Her students' engagement and interest in that moment later prompted her to rethink the annual showcase, asking students "What would you like to showcase?" rather than choosing projects herself. This seemingly small change reflects a profound shift in what it means to showcase work in her classroom; the focus of the celebration shifts from her own judgment of student work to what her students themselves want to share with others, what feels most important and meaningful to them. Her students' enthusiasm in response to both invitations reflects an investment, ownership, and accompanying engagement that Kristine believes is essential to meaningful learning. In our conversation, she explained why this feeling of investment is so important:

> Because that's where they actually start learning—when they are invested in it, when they have engaged and when they have made it something of them. When they can connect that to what they've experienced in the classroom or in school, then that's where the real power and the real magic are. Just rote learning—I can get As all day long if I regurgitate what my teacher wants. But an A doesn't really mean that I learned anything. It just means that I was a good student and I followed the rules. Learning happens when you're able to be in that moment when you think, "It means something to me. It matters to me."

Kristine told us that she often reminded herself how much students' choice and ownership over their work seemed to deepen their engagement with learning, but that—even knowing this—she recognized there were areas in her classroom and curriculum where she wasn't enabling that choice and ownership as much as she wanted to. In this vignette, we see how the changes Kristine made are part of the ongoing work of broadening her understanding and deployment of pedagogical practices that are aligned with her aspirations for students and their learning. If this process of alignment between intention and action were easy or straightforward, we would achieve it and move on. Instead, it is something we must do over and over again, every day, as teachers. Kristine has been a teacher for more than twenty years, and continues to be actively engaged in processes of reflecting on what she is doing in the classroom: thinking about her vision and values for student learning, her current pedagogical practices, and what she might do differently.

As American education researcher and theorist of teacher learning Lee Shulman wrote in a collection of essays on teaching titled *The Wisdom of Practice*, published in 2004, "One never learns to teach once and for all. It is a continuous, ongoing, constantly deepening process."[106] Among his many professional contributions (including promoting the concept of Pedagogical Content Knowledge, or PCK, in the 1980s), Shulman's work was dedicated to understanding what exactly is involved in the practice of teaching and what enables it to happen. He argued that this deepening process of change, as we see Kristine undertaking in her practice, is necessary precisely because the work of teaching is so complex, in ways that are often unrecognized and unappreciated. He argued that it is not experience alone that enables growth; it is the ability to learn from that experience, to allow it to prompt you to make a change, that enables growth.

By foregrounding learners' ideas of what is important and affording them more agency and decision-making power in the learning process, Kristine's new approach to showcasing student projects introduces more excitement into the learning environment, but also more uncertainty and unpredictability, adding to the complexity of teaching that Shulman described. When Kristine was the one choosing which projects were shown, either in a regular class or as part of a culminating public showcase, she knew what her reasons were for doing so. She determined that their quality was good and that their display had value. Now, when she invites students to decide what they want to show, she is sharing control. In addition to a general expansion of the numbers and types of work shown, many of the projects her students choose for themselves are not what Kristine would have chosen, nor even anticipated that students would want to share. She has to let go of her own criteria for what is worthy of display and embrace the value of a project being meaningful to learners on their own terms. Kristine shared that this shift felt unsettling. She described the moment of unplanned-for in-class sharing as "weird and wild," a description that aptly conveyed the absence of control she had previously exercised. But she embraced this change in the service of her broader goals and aspirations for learners.

Kristine told us about her changing ideas and practices for showcasing student work in an entirely matter-of-fact manner. To her, this kind of continual navigation between aspiration and enactment, this process of ongoing development in her classroom practice, was simply part of the work of teaching. Yet Shulman noted how vulnerable teachers can feel when engaging in this kind of experimentation, particularly teaching that honors students' own ideas about their learning:

> We also must recognize how much risk is entailed in doing the kind of teaching we are advocating, and why we must create structures within our schools that permit teachers to take those risks and then celebrate them, not bury them.[107]

When teaching is not recognized in all of its complexity, it is understandably more difficult for teachers to take these risks, to make these kinds of changes. Adopting a stance toward teaching that recognizes this complexity by embracing teaching as an iterative process enables us to purposefully and meaningfully explore our pedagogical imaginations, to create new opportunities for the weird and the wild—and the wonderful—in our classrooms.

WHAT WERE YOUR STRUGGLES?

For the past month, Janet's fourth graders have been engaged in a science unit focused on force and motion. They've been making predictions and testing their ideas by building physical models and coding digital models, simulating cars rolling down different surfaces and inclines. Throughout the unit, Janet's students have shared and discussed their models with each other. They've been getting feedback, iteratively revising their creations, and deepening their science understandings.

Now, at the end of the unit, Janet wants an opportunity for each of her students to reflect privately on their experiences—what they made, how they made it, and what the experience meant to them. Janet prepares a series of reflective prompts for her students to respond to. She handwrites the prompts across several pages, with space for her students to draw and write. She includes prompts about how they developed the vision for their project and how they felt about their evolving understandings of force and motion. She includes prompts about what parts were difficult, asking her students explicitly, "What were your struggles?"

Students handwrite their reflections in the spaces that Janet has provided. Their responses reflect the thoughtfulness and seriousness with which they took their work, their investment in making a project that engaged their own imaginations and their developing scientific understanding, and their comfort with the idea that the process of creation isn't entirely smooth. In this private space, one student writes, "My struggle mostly occurred when I was working on the loop-de-loop, because of how many angles I had to put in." Another shares, "The hardest thing to make my car realistic was to make my car not fly. I kept making very small movements with my car so I could make it realistic."

Janet also wants to give the students space to reflect on and express thoughts regarding their experience of coding as a creative medium, about what worked and what didn't work for them in the design of the project. She asks them, "Do you think coding a digital model is a good way to show that you know about forces and motion? Do you think coding allows you to be creative? Do you enjoy using coding in science?" Janet always includes a "Why?" at the end of these questions; it is a request to explain their reasoning that she hopes communicates to students that their perspective matters and also helps her reflect on her own teaching practice.

Finally, Janet includes a prompt for students to illustrate themselves working on the project. The drawings students make reflect the complexity of the creative process: the initial moment of developing a vision, the satisfaction of making something work after trying for a while ("I did it! I made my car move."), and the awareness of something that isn't working ("I need to make my car more realistic at the top of the hill."). While many of these illustrations match Janet's own observations of her students throughout the unit, there are also surprises, elements of the students' experiences and feelings that this reflective space enables them to express in ways they hadn't previously. Janet learns about the unexpected pride of one student who had quietly been making progress throughout the unit, and the secret frustration of another student who visualized her experience through a comic strip demonstrating the initial ease she felt, followed by later struggles, illustrated by her playfully frustrated destruction of her computer.

Janet's classroom is full of beautiful objects her students have created, both physical and digital, reflecting scientific concepts like force and motion, geological change, and food chains. She routinely engages her students in considering audience as they create—thinking about how their work will be received by others and how others' reactions can serve as signals of what is and isn't working in their creations. But just as important to their learning, Janet encourages the less visible process of reflection, which she organizes as a handwritten conversation between learners and their teacher. The form is quiet, intimate. The handwritten nature signals that it is for them, not for anyone else. It is an opportunity to think about the choices they have made, the development of their conceptual understanding, and their experience of learning. This is a purposeful choice, as Janet explained to us:

> We talk a lot about quality work and presentation of work, and then we talk about work that's not formal presentation work. We differentiate the two a lot by the way it was handwritten like that. If it's a very metacognitive, reflective

non-presentation tool, then I will handwrite the work, so that it's very clear that I don't mean for it to be a presentation piece. I mean for it to be something, a conversation or something, that we're keeping in.

Through the questions that Janet asks the students—what inspired their vision, what they think of coding—she is making space for them to think about what their creating means to them. As she references in the preceding quote, figuring out your own thinking is a particular kind of work that can be supported with privacy. Through the private space of handwritten reflection, Janet creates safety for students to process the challenging emotions that can accompany the creative process, such as the struggles of giving form to their ideas and the potential frustrations of not always being able to do so.

In her 2011 book *Alone Together*, American sociologist and psychologist Sherry Turkle underscored the deep need for young people to have these kinds of safe, private spaces for figuring out their thoughts and who they are. Long fascinated by the affordances of computers as an expressive medium and as environments for engaging in the complex work of identity building, Turkle's examination of what she termed *the networked life* led her to worry about the burden of digital, networked technologies. She documented the ways in which these technologies can leave us in a state of constant performance, leading us to simultaneously feel a lack of comfort with certain experiences of togetherness and with certain experiences of aloneness. As she wrote:

> My own study of the networked life has left me thinking about intimacy—about being with people in person, hearing their voices and seeing their faces, and trying to know their hearts. And it has left me thinking about solitude—the kind that refreshes and restores. Loneliness is failed solitude. To experience solitude you must be able to summon yourself by yourself; otherwise, you will only know how to be lonely.[108]

Turkle argued that both public time and private time are needed. There are times and spaces to be alone with your thoughts and there are times and spaces to engage with others. Part of what Janet is offering her students is clarity about that difference. She offers that clarity in what questions she asks them—and in how she asks those questions. The handwritten format of the prompts invites students to turn inward and to slow down. Handwritten communication feels more personal than the typed word. When we look at handwriting, we know it takes more time and effort, which lends weight and significance to what is written, for both writer and reader. Through her handwritten prompts, Janet is signaling to her students how much she values them and their thoughts, and she wants them to feel that same value for themselves and their own ideas.

In the classroom as design studio, we know how powerful it is for learners to have opportunities for public presentation, recognition, and validation of their creations. This public engagement benefits the development of ideas, as well as the development of a student's core sense of competency and contribution. As Turkle wrote about young people, "Being seen means that they are not insignificant."[109] What we are surfacing by highlighting Janet's reflection practices, and what Turkle's work surfaced, is the limitation of public presentation and engagement being the *only* way for students to see and understand their work. In learning and in life, there are things that are important that aren't for show. Janet is helping her students to develop a trust in themselves and their own perspective, so that when they do engage in the necessary work of sharing their creations and ideas with others, the responses that they receive contribute to, but do not overwhelm, their own core self.

WHAT WOULD YOU HAVE DONE IF YOU HAD MORE TIME?

Middle school technology teacher Ana notices that many of her sixth-grade students are interested in video gaming, so she creates a video game design unit that she hopes will help them develop their coding capacity. She gives general parameters for their games. Each game has to include two or more sprites, two different backgrounds, and a scoring component, and one sprite has to move. Beyond these requirements, students have total freedom in what the theme and structure are, how the program functions, and what it looks like. Students are excited about the opportunity and their games vary wildly, from animal grooming simulations to pop culture tributes. Many students choose to hand draw their own sprites and backgrounds, and one student composes his own music for his game.

Throughout the project, Ana emphasizes the importance of the creative process. She tells her students, "Document your iteration. Screenshot everything. Tell me what else you need to do. I want to see what you've learned." From the early days of the project, students develop sketches and storyboards of their games, adding those images to their documentation and writing about their process. As their game development progresses, students start taking screenshots of their code and adding it to their documentation—or screencasts of their projects in action, accompanied by writing about what is happening and what they've done. As students work, Ana moves throughout the room and checks in with them. She asks students to show her what's going on in their game, and tell her about what elements are going well and what is causing them difficulty.

At the end of the unit, Ana encourages students to reflect on the process overall. She structures that reflection with questions that are both forward- and backward-looking, and that prompt students toward their own concerns, perspectives, and judgment: "What parts of this project did you really love? What are you proud of? What do you hate? What could you have done better? What would you have done if you had more time?" In addition to informing her own understanding of them and their work, Ana draws on the documentation as a way for students to recognize their growth and appreciate their own development, saying to her students, "Look at all this work you did, and now you can show it to somebody else."

There are multiple purposes to the documenting of process and accompanying reflection that Ana structures for her students. The documentation helps Ana understand the students' work and what it means to them. She noted that some students created games that, on the surface, seemed simple, but their descriptions of their process and how they figured out their code reflected important conceptual understanding and personal growth she would not have otherwise been able to recognize. The documentation also helps validate and celebrate what learners have been able to do. Ana contrasted the games project with some earlier experiences that involved learning coding through short exercises and puzzles, after which students remarked, "I don't have anything to show for this." And finally, the documentation helps focus students on the *process* of creation as what they will take away from their learning experience, through helping them understand how they think, learn, and create. When Ana spoke with us about what was most important to her in the learning experience in her classroom, she explained: "My recurrent theme is recognizing that you're going through a process when you create something. Every single time you're doing a process. They're understanding how they learn, and how they do things." By asking them questions like "What would you have done if you had more time?," Ana is setting up her students for future learning, helping them to be cognizant of the kinds of decisions and judgments they make as they create.

The idea of asking learners about their thoughts and ideas is a key aspect of constructivism, a theory of learning based on the work of pioneering Swiss psychologist and epistemologist Jean Piaget. Much of how Piaget is taken up more broadly within education focuses on the specifics of his articulation of different stages of young people's cognitive development and, especially, his emphasis on the dynamic process by which children make sense of the world around them using their own existing thoughts and ideas, the process by which they literally construct their understanding.

Yet these insights about children's learning processes would not have been possible without another, less commonly recognized element of his contribution—one that has been noted by students of his such as Seymour Papert and Eleanor Duckworth, whose ideas have been shared elsewhere in this book. This is Piaget's assertion that the only way we can really understand children and what they think is by talking to them, in depth and at length, and listening to their responses with the utmost seriousness. The seeming simplicity of this act—asking children what they think and listening to their responses—masks its profundity, and the significance of Piaget's undertaking of it in a previously unheard of manner. As he wrote in his 1929 text, *The Child's Conception of the World*, "How many inexpressible thoughts must remain unknown so long as we restrict ourselves to observing the child without talking to him?"[110] As Ana reflected, there were things she wasn't able to understand from looking at students' projects alone, both about the projects themselves and about the learning processes that produced them, especially ways that learners had persevered in struggle, figured things out, and had grown in their understanding. She was able to surface these important insights because she asked learners directly about their process and thinking, both verbally as she moved about the room and in their written reflections.

But there is another element of the value of asking students about their thinking that Ana surfaced in our conversations with her, one that speaks to the impact that asking students these types of questions has on their ideas about themselves, as people and learners. After talking about how she wanted learners to be aware that they were going through a process in their creative work, Ana added that she wanted them to know that "they also can learn things without a teacher sitting there telling them what to learn." Here Ana is connecting her prompt for learners to reflect on their creative processes to the aspirations she holds for her students—to develop and act as autonomous beings, to see that there are things they are able to figure out and do on their own. She is asking them what they think so they can recognize how much they have within themselves.

This idea is not explicit in Piaget's earlier work, where his focus is on the substance of the thinking that is surfaced in his conversations with young people. But his research methods presume that learners have something to say about their own thinking, and in later work he more directly engaged with wanting for learners the power that Ana names here, the power of thinking for themselves, of valuing what they are able to figure out on their own. In remarks made while speaking at a conference in 1964, transcribed by his student Eleanor Duckworth, Piaget proposed:

> The principal goal of education is to create men who are capable of doing new things, not simply repeating what other generations have done—men who are creative, inventive, and discoverers . . . [who] can be critical, can verify, and not accept everything they are offered.[111]

This is what asking learners about their thinking communicates to them: that they are people capable of production and creativity, capable of developing their own ideas. In the classroom as design studio, the inclusion of reflective practices signals that we take learners and their thinking seriously and, in doing so, we encourage learners to take themselves seriously.

WHAT DO YOU SEE?

Jordan's classroom is a space of experimentation and exploration. He provides students with materials—digital tools for coding and animation, a green screen for recording, scissors and hot glue, electronics and conductive tape. And then he invites them to create, telling them to help themselves to anything in the room, except his desk. As students engage in these explorations, Jordan quietly circulates throughout the room, checking in with students about how things are going, what they are thinking about, and what they have made of the materials.

As he does this, he is also taking photographs of the projects, of the learners. His photos tend to capture small moments that might pass by unnoticed in the busyness of the classroom. One image shows a student holding a wire for another as they build something together. Another image reveals two students, who don't normally interact, thoughtfully pointing to a computer screen and discussing a digital animation one has created. Another image documents four students sitting with puzzled looks on their faces as they debug a device they have built using simple circuits.

With these photos, Jordan asks his students, their parents, the broader school community, and himself, "What do you see?" He shares photos directly with students, displaying collages at the beginning of class to celebrate what has happened and set a tone for the day, and reviews them with students in individual meetings to prompt discussion about their experiences and goals for the future. He posts updates to social media after class so family members and friends can see what learners have been up to. For the school's monthly assemblies, instead of giving out individual awards as other teachers do, Jordan creates a slideshow of photographs to make his students' work and process visible to the school at large. And, at the end of the year, he shares a curated collection of the slideshow images with students' families and friends, so others can appreciate students' learning and creating from throughout the year.

Jordan told us that he is always taking photographs of students and the classroom. He loves that way of engaging with the world around him and he sees the photographs as essential material for understanding the work that learners are doing. Longtime Reggio Emilia educator and learning theorist Carlina Rinaldi helps us appreciate these photographs as part of the important documentation of learning in the classroom. Rinaldi offered an alternative vision for the use of documentation in schools, where it has typically been reviewed after the work is done, as an aid to evaluation. Instead, as Jordan does here, Rinaldi described documentation as an essential part of the learning process, as a means of constructing meaning about who the learner is, and what the learning is, in ways that can inform the choices that are made moving forward. Documentation is a tool for the kinds of listening that are so central to learning environments—the teacher listening to the students, and students listening to each other and to themselves. As Rinaldi explained in a 2001 essay included in the edited volume *Making Learning Visible: Children as Individual and Group Learners*:

> Documentation, therefore, is seen as visible listening, as the construction of traces (through notes, slides, videos, and so on) that not only testify to the children's learning paths and processes, but also make them possible because they are visible. For us this means making visible, and thus possible, the relationships that are the building blocks of knowledge.[112]

The moments that Jordan captures in his photographs—learners helping one another, puzzling through difficulties in construction, expressing interest and excitement in what others have done—are signature elements of student-directed exploration in the classroom as design studio. By making such moments visible, Jordan legitimates them as moments of learning, communicating their value to all in the learning community and inviting this kind of learning to flourish, both within and beyond his classroom.

Jordan uses these photographs to ask the question "What do you see?" of many different people, prompting multiple processes of reflection on the learning that is happening. First, Jordan asks this question of his students, helping learners construct essential meanings about themselves, especially about their capacity for expression, for navigating the challenges of open-ended work, about their value and contribution as human beings. As he explained:

> I just want the kids to feel good about what they made. When they show it off, and you acknowledge it, validate it, they're going to feel good about themselves. And they're going to want to keep doing more. I'd put something on social media, in the middle of the day, about a kid's project. Then I was out back at dismissal, and I saw the parent, and the parent saw me, and we started talking about it. And the kid wasn't out there yet. So when the kid got to the parent, there was already, like, "I saw what you did today!" The kid started talking. Just those opportunities, using social media as a platform for the kids to feel good about themselves, and then talk more about everything.

Through his photographs, Jordan is offering his students material for constructing a narrative of who they are, of what they've done, of support for one another, perseverance in the face of challenge, their identity as creators. Rinaldi, noting that young people rarely want to be anonymous, argued that part of the power of documentation, and documentation as a form of listening, is that it "legitimates us" and "gives us visibility."[113] Jordan legitimates learners and their work when he uses photographs to invite his students' families to see what they've done. As he notes in the preceding quote, this greater visibility helps learners develop confidence in themselves and also helps them talk more about what they are learning and making in the classroom, which supports their future learning.

Jordan is also using the photographs to ask himself the question "What do you see?" As Rinaldi explained, the value of the meaning-making work that goes on through documentation, and the prompt to reflection, is not just for learners, but also for those doing the documentation. Jordan uses the photographs as an opportunity for his own reflection and learning. The photographs tell him something about what is happening in his classroom and what it might mean. In curating photographs for a slideshow, he noticed the photograph of the two students who don't usually interact talking animatedly and interestedly about what one of them was coding. He hadn't realized the significance of this moment when he had taken the photo, but seeing it later, he theorized that engagement in expressive, open-ended work enabled this unexpected, and unexpectedly meaningful, social connection. When he was putting together photographs to show us his classroom, he noticed that many of them, more than he would have anticipated, involved learners in screen-free coding activities and he reflected on the value of those kinds of activities for supporting programming work.

Jordan's openness to what the photographs can tell him about learners, about what is going on in his classroom, his openness to things he might not have realized, is reflective of the deeply responsive character of his teaching, of his embrace of the listening that Rinaldi advocated. As she wrote:

> Listening is not easy. . . . It requires openness to change. It demands that we have clearly in mind the value of the unknown and that we are able to overcome the sense of emptiness and precariousness we experience whenever our certainties are questioned.[114]

Jordan engages in a continual process of inviting his students into activities, inviting them to explore with materials, informed by his sense of what might be valuable for them as learners and as people. Given the uncertainty inherent to the exploratory nature of these activities, he is attentive to how the students respond and the meaning they are making of it. This embrace of uncertainty itself, along with the other specific qualities of learning that Jordan surfaces in his photographs—an emphasis on collaboration and process over individualized achievement, moments of thinking things through and figuring out what to do next—are qualities that can be more difficult to make visible, to celebrate publicly. When Jordan shares these photographs with others who might not necessarily think about learning in the same way, and asks them, "What do you see?," he communicates a powerful message about what he sees as valuable in the learning environment, and in doing so, makes such learning more possible in the future.

III

DIRECTIONS

WHAT DID WE SEE?

In the final story of part II, we learn about Jordan's practice of visual documentation in his classroom. Guided by the question *What do you see?* Jordan invites his students, the wider community, and himself to consider what they are noticing about learners and their ideas, about their self-directed project work and the broader ideas about learning it reflects. In this book, we have endeavored to share our own documentation—of twenty-five classrooms and teachers and the hundreds of students they represent—in this same spirit. Each story has rendered a vision of what's possible in practice, each in conversation with a theoretical idea to highlight what is powerful and important in this learning. But there is more happening within each story and across the entire collection of stories. And so we will now step back here, creating space for sharing what we see within and across this collection.

Recalling the invitation from the beginning of this book, in the blank space below (or another suitable place), we invite you to make a list of ideas, themes, or questions in response to the prompt: *What did you see?*

The writing of this book has itself been a process of asking ourselves, over and over again, *What did we see?* As we listened to recordings of the conversations with teachers, combed through teachers' reflective journals, and read notes from classroom observations, we felt certain that the stories we were developing from these source materials put in conversation with theoretical texts were showing us something important, something we wanted to share with others about how teachers support self-direction. But we struggled to define what that something was. To make sense of what we were seeing, we read each story together and wrote statements about the most important things we saw. Separately, we each took that set of almost two hundred statements and worked to identify central ideas about the classroom as design studio. Karen worked systematically, comparing and sorting the statements, and developing a set of themes. Sarah worked holistically, reading through the set of statements all together, taking handwritten notes, and reflecting on what ideas felt most important. When we met to talk through what we had seen, we discovered that these divergent paths led us to the same place, a remarkably clear and early agreement between us about what the stories were offering, about what characterized the classroom as design studio.

For us, when we look across these stories of teachers and their classrooms, we see teachers united in their aspirations for learner self-direction, and in their beliefs that open-ended projects, created in community, can serve as a rich context for those aspirations to flourish. These teachers want the students in their classrooms to trust in themselves, as people with ideas, as people who can figure things out. They want their students to have an increased sense of reliance on themselves—for deciding what is important, for knowing how to do things, for judging what works and what does not.

And we see what it looks like for teachers to support this learner self-direction. As we discussed earlier, in part I of the book, it has been difficult within educational research and practice to understand self-direction and support as mutually reinforcing rather than in tension. Self-direction has often been described in terms of the absence of traditional supports and structures, such as *not* telling students what to do and how to do it, or *not* designing situations in which students produce materials and outcomes exactly as the teacher has intended. It has been harder to describe what it looks like to engage in teaching that centers learners and their own ideas.

In this collection of stories, we see the importance of teacher presence in supporting self-direction. We see it in the interactions and activities that they purposefully employ in their learning environments and learning experiences, in their creation of a distinct culture of learning in the classroom, as well as their attentiveness and responsiveness to their students.

ASKING QUESTIONS

Across all of these stories, we saw one essential practice that teachers use to support learners' self-direction: asking learners questions. And these questions felt different in important ways from the questions young people might expect at school. Instead of questions with answers that the teacher already knows or that textbooks could readily supply, the questions we heard teachers asking started with the learners themselves. Teachers asked learners what they wanted to make and do, what they thought, what was important to them. These questions communicated teachers' genuine curiosity about learners' work and ideas, and—powerfully—teachers' belief that learners have important and valuable ideas to share about what is worth learning and how to learn it.

Asking these questions helped teachers understand how to honor students' selves in the classroom, to connect learners to one another when it was useful, and to provide forms of help that would advance learners' own goals. We saw teachers listening, thoughtfully and seriously, to students' replies. And we saw teachers acting on what they heard; these questions enabled teachers to be responsive to their students and the ideas they shared. This responsiveness sometimes involved acting on something small, such as hearing from a learner about what they want to do and then trying to find the right resource to support them, or hearing about where they are getting stuck and joining them in their explorations. But it sometimes involved bigger changes, such as stopping the usual progression of the day to attend to more immediate needs, or changing the overall design of a project.

Again and again, we saw how the practice of asking questions—that teachers asked questions, what they were asking through those questions, and how they made use of what they learned—served as the starting point for supporting student self-direction, for supporting the intellectually rich and personally meaningful learning of the classroom as design studio. We saw how teachers' questions were used to express and sustain six core commitments:

honoring ideas, interests, and identities;
inviting decisions;
encouraging trying;
cultivating connections;
offering help and affirmation; and
highlighting process.

We do not present this as a checklist of things to do, but rather a collection of core commitments that inform and interact with one another in the service of supporting self-direction. Each of these commitments is grounded in a desire to help learners believe that they are capable of self-direction, experience what it feels like to exercise self-direction, and develop greater capacity and motivation for exercising self-direction in the future. In concert, guided by the essential practice of asking questions, these six core commitments provide a foundation for the classroom as design studio, as we will now describe.

HONORING IDEAS, INTERESTS, AND IDENTITIES

We saw teachers honoring learners' ideas, interests, and identities by structuring activities, assignments, and projects that invited students to express themselves, to make personal connections to the work. This ranged from completely open-ended learning opportunities (for example, students creating whatever they wanted) to opportunities that were more constrained (for example, by subject matter goals, such as students exploring the mathematical concept of fractals by programming their own visual trees). But independent of the overall degree of freedom, we saw how teachers communicated to learners, implicitly and explicitly, that they should make the work their own. Honoring learners' ideas, interests, and identities also meant teachers expressing interest in and concern for their students as human beings. Teachers recognized that it can be hard to do the work if you haven't been sleeping well, or if you're fighting with your best friend, or if you've heard something scary on the news. We saw how teachers asked students about their lives within and beyond the classroom, listening to the responses, and validating learners' thinking and feeling by responsively offering support.

INVITING DECISIONS

From this starting place of recognizing what was important to learners, we saw teachers invite students to make decisions about their learning. Students had space to decide—meaningfully, consequentially—what they worked on and how they worked on it. Teachers then supported the decisions students made for themselves, even (and perhaps especially) when the decisions were different from the ones that teachers might have made on their behalf. We saw how teachers' commitment to inviting decisions encouraged them to think creatively and expansively about opportunities for students to make choices and exercise control over what they were doing and how they were doing it. This included choices that were traditionally the exclusive province of the teacher, such as assessment of work quality and methods of work presentation. And, given that many students were unfamiliar with having the power and responsibility to make consequential decisions about their learning, we saw teachers offering explanations and engaging in discussions about why making such decisions is important, in the service of helping students trust their capacity to make those decisions for themselves.

ENCOURAGING TRYING

What was both wonderful and a little intimidating about the type of self-directed work and learning we saw in these classrooms is that no one—learners or teachers—knew exactly what would happen. Each student was unique and each project experience was unique. A learner may have immediately had an idea for what they want to work on, or they may have struggled with developing a concept. A learner might have known exactly what they want to create, but might not yet have had the tools, experience, and knowledge to make their concept real. In response to this environment of endemic uncertainty and struggle, we saw teachers encouraging their students to try, and try again, communicating to them that the process of trying would yield productive learning, particularly if it involved moments of challenge and failure. Cultures of trying were manifested through what teachers said and how they themselves responded to uncertainty, demonstrating interest and curiosity about the unknown. And cultures of trying were further supported in how teachers designed activities and class sessions. A key element of these classrooms was allocating time for exploration, experimentation, and iteration. We saw how teachers offered learners more time for these activities than is often given in classrooms, creating room for all parts of the creative process: students had time to develop initial ideas, to wrestle with how to make those ideas real, to dive into an approach (and then possibly change direction), to struggle, to connect to others and other resources as needed, and to revise and iterate in response.

CULTIVATING CONNECTIONS

Across these classrooms, we saw teachers supporting students in pursuing their self-directed learning by helping them explore ideas that mattered to them, make decisions about their own work, and experiment enthusiastically. Everything that teachers were doing communicated to students: *Your ideas are important.* But we also saw two concurrent—and equally powerful—messages from teachers: *Other people's ideas are important*, and, *together, our ideas can mutually support and strengthen each other.* Even as teachers were sharply focused on nurturing learners' own ideas, what they cared about and what was important to them, we saw teachers emphasizing to learners that their classmates were one of the most important resources that they could draw upon to support their own ideas. In these classrooms, individual work was, profoundly, a product of collective action, with peers offering each other inspiration, collaboration, and appreciative audience. To support these interactions, we saw how teachers found opportunities to direct learners' attention to one another, such as displaying work and highlighting what learners in the classroom had done. Teachers also frequently positioned themselves as one learner among the many, modeling in their own behavior and interactions a genuine interest in what students had done and a sincere desire to learn from them. In doing so, we saw teachers create classroom cultures that were deeply collaborative rather than competitive, with a shared sense of responsibility among students, a shared intellectual and emotional investment in each other's work and learning.

OFFERING HELP AND AFFIRMATION

We saw how teachers were thoughtful and purposeful about how they designed and structured classroom projects and activities that offered students accessible ways into self-directed work, carefully attending to learners' needs, developmental and otherwise. In moments of unproductive struggle, when learners were unable to progress on their own, we saw teachers directly intervene in a variety of ways, while still preserving and encouraging learner agency and autonomy. Teachers offered potential resources, questions to help reframe student thinking, or suggestions for finding a different approach. Teachers wanted to help their students feel less dependent on them as teachers, but they knew that to feel independent, to exercise self-direction throughout the learning process, students needed to feel capable. In response, they offered affirmation—warm and enthusiastic, not superficially congratulatory. Teachers affirmed to learners that they were capable of this kind of work, that they had wonderful ideas, that they would be able to figure things out, that they could help others. This affirmation was tacitly communicated through the design of the activities, asking students to dream and pursue projects that mattered to them. But it was also offered directly. We saw teachers affirming students through encouraging language, through celebration of their work, and most importantly, through paying attention—taking learners seriously by watching, listening, and responding.

HIGHLIGHTING PROCESS

We saw teachers encouraging students to make what they want to make and taking seriously what students' creations mean to them. But we also saw teachers calling attention to the importance of process—the process of creation in the particular moment, and the broader process of learning, of students' evolving identities as creators. Teachers highlighted process in a variety of ways, from celebrating works in progress, to inviting students to reflect on what they had made, what they thought of it, and what they might do differently in the future. This often involved making students' work and learning visible, both within the classroom and beyond, so that learners and others could better recognize what had happened and think about what it might mean. By encouraging students to pay attention to process, teachers invited them to step back and appreciate their individual growth, their evolving capability as self-directed learners, and to think about the implications for their future learning. Self-directed learning isn't a moment or a discrete activity; it's a way of seeing yourself.

As we conclude our shared writing, we are conscious that this book has been our own collaborative, self-directed learning experience—and we have often found ourselves reflected in the struggles faced by the students about whom we have been writing. As we saw with these students and have experienced with our own students, it can be hard to end things you care about. *How do you know when you're done? How do you know if you did what you were trying to do?* Sometimes you run out of time or up against a deadline. Sometimes you exhaust the ideas or yourself. Sometimes you just know or feel that what you've made is complete, it's done—or at least done enough for now.

Embracing the advice we heard from these teachers, to whom we are so profoundly grateful: everything is iterative. We've shared what we've seen and learned so far, and we hope that this collective description of the classroom as design studio has offered you ideas for supporting self-direction—perhaps affirming existing practices or inspiring new connections. But any particular moment of ending isn't important in and of itself; we hold it in relation to where we've been and where we're going, to the learning we've experienced and the learning that awaits us. When we return to these ideas, whether in a week, a month, or a few years, we'll be different and differently positioned, ready to see new things and pursue new directions.

WHAT CAN WE DO?

The first time I tried to write these thoughts was a year ago. Karen and I were finishing our first full draft of this book, realizing an embodiment of ideas we had been thinking about and talking about for many years. And I was getting ready to return to classroom teaching after a decade away, after doctoral studies and an unplanned foray into postdoctoral research that fortuitously provided the opportunity to collaborate on the book. I was excited to get back to a core part of myself that I had missed (terribly, viscerally) during those years.

I had been so inspired by the teachers in this collection, listening to their voices as they described fantastic projects that combined substantive interdisciplinary ideas with space for individual expression, as they talked about how they supported students in finding their own ideas, in sharing those ideas with others, as they facilitated meaningful connections within the classroom that sparked new thinking. And I had been so inspired by the theory I had read in doctoral studies and for this book, descriptions of how to provide rich contexts in which learners can develop their own ideas about how the world works, or reimaginings of interactions between teachers and students, getting away from limiting conceptions of the teacher as the one who knows and the student as the one who does not, moving toward collective, collaborative investigation of ideas that learners themselves find meaningful. I was excited to be different than I had been before, to take all of these ideas about what felt most important in learning and create a classroom community with more room for individual expression and open-ended exploration, with more weight given to learners' own ideas and ways of doing things.

I was also worried. I was worried about some practical things that had to do with being rusty, like what to do on the first day and how to establish routines. Those elements might feel challenging at first but I knew the stress would fade with time. Yet I had a deeper worry. I was worried—in a way that felt shameful somehow, that I didn't want to speak out loud—that the dissonance would be too great. I was worried that it was just a fantasy that I could return to the classroom informed and enriched by my time in academia. I was worried that it would be too upsetting to have to engage in practices I didn't agree with, to encounter ideas about children and learning that ran counter to values I hold dear, values cemented by the work on this project. I was worried that, instead of being motivated by the ideals I had encountered, the distance between those ideals and reality would be too great, too overwhelming, too discouraging, precisely because my sense of the ideals was stronger, clearer.

In the year to come, my own practice, my own self, were very far from what I would have wanted them to be. I was hired to teach fourth grade in a diverse Title I school in the Boston area thirty-six hours before the new school year started. I began behind and never caught up as I worked to learn new curricula and new assessment systems, and to establish relationships with families and students while just trying to be prepared for the next day. Like all teachers, my preparation time was laughably inadequate to the demands of teaching—forty-five minutes to plan for the other five hours, forty-five minutes that was really thirty-five minutes after walking the students to their specialist teacher and picking them up at the end. And, like many teachers experience, I had young children at home, and would be up at 2:00 a.m. holding them, and then up again a few short hours later to make lunches and get out the door. I couldn't work the long (unpaid) hours I had done earlier in my career, hours that helped to compensate for the lack of structures needed to support teaching as intellectual work. I was tired all the time, it was hard to find a moment to eat, and I was less patient and more irritable than I wanted to be. I struggled to choose the most productive things to focus on in the occasionally stolen moment for thought. I felt my classroom was endlessly messy no matter how hard I tried to make it different.

I was right that there would be a great chasm between my vision of the classroom and what I would be able to actualize in practice. And I was completely wrong that the distance would mean having to either turn away from the vision or from the practice. Amid this chaos and messiness—both inside and around me—I thought about what it meant to teach and learn in the classroom as design studio *all* the time. I thought about it as I was biking to work early in the morning, and washing dishes late at night. These ideas were balm to my soul when it had been an especially hard day and I was feeling angry and frustrated, with myself, with others, with the structural conditions of teaching and learning that invite overly simplistic and reductivist solutions to complex problems. I would think about Ursula Franklin and Carlina Rinaldi talking about resisting education on a production model, about Karl Weick and Donald Schön reminding us to allow for uncertainty rather than close it off, and I would feel calmer, able to recognize what was going on, and what was making things feel so frustrating. These ideas were fuel, energizing me to keep going, exciting me about the possibilities of each new day because it was another opportunity to be with the students, to help them feel, as teachers like Kelly and Benjamin so beautifully described, that their ideas had weight. I was excited to go in the next day because I wanted to talk to them about what they were thinking and feeling, to sit down with them, like Penny did, and work through a problem together.

And these ideas were guidance, helping me make decisions about what to focus on, what to prioritize, what to try when things (inevitably) didn't work as planned. When I became conscious that my interactions with certain students were too focused on compliance, too much me telling them what to do, and I could feel them retreating from learning, closing in on themselves, Tamara and Audre Lorde reminded me that I should try to hear their real voices. I would work to structure situations in which students could express their needs in their own terms, as Karina and Nel Noddings described, where I could follow the guidance of Nathan and Friedrich Froebel in hearing what they were drawn to and being led by that. When I could feel that I was trying to pull the students toward a specific understanding, a specific outcome, that my own agenda was dominating and they were being dragged along with it, without real understanding or connection, Jess and Richard Ryan and Edward Deci, Ana and Ursula Franklin, reminded me to give them space to make it their own, to trust that their own ideas, while different from my own, had value, and they needed to feel that value. On the many days when I was overwhelmed by all the things I needed to figure out, about reading groups and math intervention, and hadn't been able to, Andrea and bell hooks reminded me that good things would happen in learning if I focused on enjoying being with the students in the room, responding to them in the expressions of their own joys and interests. And, always, when I could feel myself falling into asking questions that I knew the answer to, I thought about Neil Postman and Charles Weingartner, and about all the beautiful questions from teachers that frame this collection—*What do you think? What are you trying to do? What does this mean to you?*—questions that always brought me closer to actually understanding my students' thinking, to connecting to them as human beings, and thus, to supporting them in their real growth and development.

The fact that you can't meet an ideal is not a reason to reject it; it's a reason to embrace it, and hold onto it. That teachers are overwhelmed and undersupported, that our work is challenging, that we don't have enough time, is almost universally acknowledged. But, too often, the response is to give us things to do, not things to think with, to see ideas as a luxury we can't afford because we need practical things that we can do the next day. In a situation of limited resources, in a situation of limited time, when you can't possibly do all the things that you want to do, ideas are what help you figure out what is important, what really matters. And ideas are what help you navigate when things go awry, as they invariably will in an endeavor as complex as learning.

Throughout the year I wondered whether there was a way to talk more directly to my students about these things I was thinking about. We did often talk about ideas about learning, about not being afraid of not knowing, about asking questions, but I struggled for the right language, for something punchy and brief that they could hold on to. This quest took on greater urgency in the spring, as many students expressed anxiety about the statewide standardized testing we had to do, that they had experienced as third graders. Despite my assertions that there were no personal consequences for them, that the information from the testing was to inform us as teachers and the district as a whole about what students were learning and what they still needed to work on, both of which were true, they said over and over again that they were worried they would do badly, that they would fail. I could see two things clearly. The first was that, even though I might think much of the content on the assessments is valuable, even though I might agree with the broader need for standardized assessments that enable schools, districts, and states to know whether they are attending to learning for all students, I couldn't keep such assessments from reinforcing an idea of learning as trying to find the right answer that someone else has determined. And, second, that anxiety about finding that right answer that someone else has determined was so pernicious and destructive that it got in the way of real learning. I could see so clearly how students' minds closed when they were focused on being right and wrong, how I couldn't get to their actual understanding because of this wall that went up.

And so I tried, each week, to frame our work with one of the quotes from a theorist in this collection. I would introduce each quote with a bit about the theorist, who they were, what they were thinking about or trying to figure out, and editorialize a bit about why the ideas felt so important to me. I shared with them Sherry Turkle on summoning yourself by yourself, Seymour Papert on fixing things, John Dewey on letting go of the inclination to win amounts of knowledge, Eleanor Duckworth on having the confidence to try out your ideas, and Jacques Rancière on believing you have something to say and communicate. Like so many of the things I tried over the course of the year, it didn't totally work, but was also meaningful and I was glad I did it. One day, during math, we were talking about recognizing fractions as equivalent. One student began to share an idea and then hesitated, saying, "I'm not sure this is right." A student in front of her turned around, threw her hands up, and said, "That's okay, just remember what Eleanor Duckworth said," and encouraged her colleague to continue her thought.

Karen began this book by offering the classroom as design studio as metaphor, as thing to think with, not as prescription. Throughout the past year, I thought about the image of the design studio, about working together and creating together, even as my own practice was very far from providing for the kinds of open-ended projects described by the teachers in this collection. Mostly my students and I were reading and talking, solving math problems and sharing our thinking. Yet, even in those more traditional forms of learning, when the thing we were building was something like an understanding of multiplication as repeated addition or an articulation of the theme in a piece of literature, it mattered very much that I was trying to reach toward creation in community, to take seriously students' own thinking, to encourage them to take seriously each other's thinking, to try, as hard as I could, to get away from an idea of learning as a search for the right answer someone else has determined. But, also, I love talking to students about their reading, I love sitting with them as they solve a math problem. As teachers, we all have different ways of doing and being, and the ideas presented here do not presume one pedagogical style, one single mode of engagement. I look forward to learning how to design more for open-ended creation in the years to come, having seen how beautifully projects can open up space for learners' ideas, for connection between learners, for deepening understanding. But I will also continue to make sense of the metaphor of the classroom as design studio in ways that resonate with who I am as an individual, that feel comfortable and connected to me, just as we hope readers may do.

I am excited about the school year to come, excited to try again next year, to hold these ideas with me in my messy reality. Whatever else happens, I know I can ask learners questions—about themselves, their work, their thinking—and listen seriously to their responses, as we work together to understand more, and do more, than we have done before.

ACKNOWLEDGMENTS

FROM BOTH OF US

The heart of this book is the work of the participating teachers, who shared so much of their time and themselves. Their participation in this research involved an enormous amount of work, on top of their demanding teaching responsibilities: meeting for interviews at lunches, during preps, and on vacations, thoughtfully gathering and annotating artifacts of learning throughout the year, navigating the bureaucracies of having researchers in their classrooms. And they were also generous, selfless, and fearless in helping us learn from the day-to-day joys and complexities of their work. To all our participating teachers: Thank you for your insights and your creativity, for showing us what is possible. You offer inspiration to us in our desire to create more spaces in which learners are seen, heard, and supported in the enactment of their own beautiful ideas.

This book would not have been possible without the research efforts of Laura Peters and Jane Kang. They did an extraordinary amount of logistical, cognitive, and emotional work in organizing, pursuing, and analyzing interviews and classroom observations, asking questions and making note of details that were so essential to us later. Both Laura and Jane have themselves been classroom teachers, and the seriousness and thoughtfulness of their engagement in this research reflected a beautiful collegial attention—a profound love of and respect for the classrooms they encountered. Laura had been involved in thinking about this project even before it was a project, and brought never-ending enthusiasm for and persistence in helping turn early questions about self-direction in K–12 classrooms into a tangible research process.

We would like to thank the many graduate students at HGSE, members and friends of the Creative Computing Lab, who enthusiastically jumped in to help us grapple with as yet unarticulated ideas about which we felt very passionate, giving their time and attention to various stages of the analytic process. Our faculty colleague Steve Seidel lent his invaluable perspective as an artist, teacher, and thinker to reading the manuscript and providing generous feedback that supported us in communicating our ideas more clearly.

Many thanks to Mitch Resnick for generously composing the Foreword. As is likely clear from other parts of the book, Mitch has offered inspiration and support for this work in ways that cannot be sufficiently described here.

This work was supported financially through a gift from Siegel Family Endowment. We are grateful for David Siegel's steadfast commitment to creative computer science learning experiences for all young learners and their teachers, and the trust he placed in the people and ideas of the Creative Computing Lab with his support.

Finally, we are grateful to the anonymous reviewers, who generously read and responded to our work, and for the phenomenal support of the MIT Press, including Julia Collins, Kathleen Caruso, and especially Susan Buckley. From the beginning, Susan understood our vision for the project and helped us realize that vision as we worked to make it legible to others.

FROM SARAH

Karen, writing this book with you has been an inexpressible joy—in the profound experience of collaboration, in the depth of intellectual exploration, in the exhilaration of figuring out what we were building as we were building it. I am so grateful to you for these ideas, which I will carry with me, always, and which were born out of your radical commitment to student self-direction and your unwavering conviction in the making and creation of artifacts as sites of meaningful learning. Thank you.

To the students, past and present, with whom I have had the privilege to work—writing this book has given me clearer and more substantive ways to understand and appreciate how precious our time together is. Every day, as I think about all the elements of the learning environment I have yet to realize, I also think about how happy I am to be there with you.

FROM KAREN

As I often remind my students, for whom I have enormous love and appreciation for the endless inspiration they offer me: creative work is intellectually and emotionally demanding. It is hard. There will be struggle. That's what makes having wonderful collaborators, like those we've already thanked, so essential. I feel especially grateful to my two most important creative collaborators in this work: Sarah Blum-Smith and Jeff Hawson.

Jeff: You experienced this book long before Sarah and I shared even a single page with you, given your proximity, in our shared home office, to my many online meetings with Sarah. Thank you for being on this journey with us, for demonstrating such profound, detailed care for the expression of these ideas and for so selflessly giving your time in helping us advance this work. For more than twenty-five years you have recognized my obsessions—never discouraging them, always finding ways to beautifully and productively amplify them.

Sarah: Over our many years together, before and throughout this book, I have learned so much from you about reading, about writing, about what a creative partnership can be. Throughout this process, I have often thought about what you must be like with your young students. I love to think about how seriously you take their ideas, listening curiously, generously, supportively, helping them navigate the struggles of bringing their ideas into the world, just as I have experienced, benefited from, and appreciated in working with you. Thank you so much—I love what we have created, but more importantly, I have loved, truly, creating this with you.

NOTES

PART I

1. *Teaching as a Subversive Activity* was also the inspiration for the participatory tactic of inviting readers to write in this book.

2. Neil Postman and Charles Weingartner, *Teaching as a Subversive Activity* (New York: Delta, 1971), 19.

3. Postman and Weingartner, *Teaching as a Subversive Activity*, 65–66.

4. Seymour Papert, *Mindstorms: Children, Computers, and Powerful Ideas* (New York: Basic Books, 1980); Seymour Papert, *The Children's Machine: Rethinking School in the Age of the Computer* (New York: Basic Books, 1993), 142.

5. Donald A. Schön, *The Design Studio: An Exploration of Its Traditions and Potentials* (London: RIBA Publications, 1985), 6; Meredith Davis, *Teaching Design: A Guide to Curriculum and Pedagogy for College Design Faculty and Teachers Who Use Design in Their Classrooms* (New York: Allworth, 2017), 81; Steven Faerm, *Introduction to Design Education: Theory, Research, and Practical Applications for Educators* (New York: Routledge, 2023), 119–122.

6. Chris Fahnoe and Punya Mishra, "Do 21st Century Learning Environments Support Self-Directed Learning? Middle School Students' Response to an Intentionally Designed Learning Environment," in *Proceedings of Society for Information Technology & Teacher Education International Conference 2013*, ed. Ron McBride and Michael Searson (New Orleans: Association for the Advancement of Computing in Education [AACE], 2013), 3131–3139; Cindy E. Hmelo-Silver, "Problem-Based Learning: What and How Do Students Learn?," *Educational Psychology Review* 16 (2004), 235–266.

7. John Holt, *How Children Fail* (New York: Pitman, 1964); John Holt, *How Children Learn* (New York: Pitman, 1967); John Holt, *Freedom and Beyond* (New York: Penguin, 1972); Carl Rogers, *Freedom to Learn* (Columbus, OH: Charles E. Merrill, 1969).

8. Malcolm Knowles, *Self-Directed Learning: A Guide for Learners and Teachers* (Chicago: Follett, 1975), 10–11. Italics in the original.

9. Donald Mocker and George Spear, "Lifelong Learning: Formal, Nonformal, Informal, and Self-Directed," *Information Series*, no. 241 (1982): 1–26.

10. Stephen Brookfield, "Self-Directed Adult Learning: A Critical Paradigm," *Adult Education Quarterly* 35, no. 2 (1984): 59–71.

11. Adele Chené, "The Concept of Autonomy in Adult Education: A Philosophical Discussion," *Adult Education Quarterly* 34, no. 1 (1983): 38–47.

12. National Research Council, *How People Learn: Brain, Mind, Experience, and School: Expanded Edition* (Washington, DC: The National Academies Press, 2000).

13. John Dewey, *Experience and Education* (New York: Kappa Delta Pi, 1938); Paulo Freire, *Pedagogy of Freedom: Ethics, Democracy, and Civic Courage* (Lanham, MD: Rowman & Littlefield, 1998).

14. Allen M. Tough, *Learning Without a Teacher: A Study of Tasks and Assistance During Adult Self-Teaching* (Toronto: Ontario Institute for Studies in Education, 1967), 29–30.

15. Chené, "The Concept of Autonomy"; Donn Randy Garrison, "Self-Directed Learning: Toward a Comprehensive Model," *Adult Education Quarterly* 48, no. 1 (1997): 18–33.

16. Stephen Brookfield, "Self-Directed Learning: A Critical Review of Research," *New Directions for Adult and Continuing Education* 25 (1985): 5–16; Merryl Hammond and Rob Collins, *Self-Directed Learning: Critical Practice* (London: Kogan Page, 1991).

17. National Research Council, *How People Learn.*

18. Cindy E. Hmelo-Silver, Ravit Golan Duncan, and Clark A. Chinn, "Scaffolding and Achievement in Problem-Based and Inquiry Learning: A Response to Kirschner, Sweller, and Clark," *Educational Psychologist* 42, no. 2 (2007): 99–107; Paul A. Kirschner, John Sweller, and Richard E. Clark, "Why Minimal Guidance During Instruction Does Not Work: An Analysis of the Failure of Constructivist, Discovery, Problem-Based, Experiential, and Inquiry-Based Teaching," *Educational Psychologist* 41, no. 2 (2006): 75–86.

19. Sigmund Tobias and Thomas M. Duffy, "The Success or Failure of Constructivist Instruction: An Introduction," in *Constructivist Instruction: Success or Failure?*, ed. Sigmund Tobias and Thomas M. Duffy (London: Taylor & Francis Group, 2009), 3–10.

20. David Jonassen, "Reconciling a Human Cognitive Architecture," in Tobias and Duffy, eds., *Constructivist Instruction*, 13–33.

21. Karen Brennan, "How Kids Manage Self-Directed Programming Projects: Strategies and Structures," *Journal of the Learning Sciences* 30, nos. 4–5 (2021): 576–610; Daniel L. Schwartz and John D. Bransford, "A Time for Telling," *Cognition and Instruction* 16, no. 4 (1998): 475–522.

22. Kenneth Burke, *The Philosophy of Literary Form* (New York: Vintage, 1957), 253.

PART II

1. With generous support and understanding from our editors at the MIT Press, we have departed from standard formatting conventions for quotes. We considered multiple factors in deciding on the formatting of each quote—length, independent legibility, the power of the idea—and ultimately made a decision that was based on intuition, rather than algorithm. We have chosen to present as block quotes a number of shorter fragments from both teachers and theorists, rather than integrate them into the body of the paragraph. This formatting is done to draw special attention to these words and the meaning that they hold, and to offer them to you for your own reflection.

2. Maria Montessori, *Spontaneous Activity in Education*, trans. Florence Simmons (New York: Stokes, 1917), 182.

3. Maria Montessori, *The Montessori Method*, trans. Anne E. George (New York: Schocken, 1912), 87–88. Italics in the original.

4. Holt, *Freedom and Beyond*, 70.

5. Holt, 73.

6. Holt, 70.

7. John Holt, *How Children Fail*, rev. ed. (New York: Delacorte, 1982), 293.

8. Karl E. Weick, *Sensemaking in Organizations* (Thousand Oaks, CA: Sage, 1995), 54.

9. Weick, *Sensemaking in Organizations*, 55.

10. Karl E. Weick, "Administering Education in Loosely Coupled Schools," *Phi Delta Kappan* 63, no. 10 (June 1982): 674.

11. Weick, "Administering Education," 675.

12. "100 languages," Reggio Children, https://www.reggiochildren.it/en/reggio-emilia-approach/100-linguaggi-en/.

13. Carlina Rinaldi, *In Dialogue with Reggio Emilia: Listening, Researching and Learning*, 2nd ed. (New York: Routledge, 2021), 158.

14. Rinaldi, *In Dialogue with Reggio Emilia*, 104.

15. Eleanor Duckworth, "The Having of Wonderful Ideas," *Harvard Educational Review* 42, no. 2 (May 1972): 218.

16. Duckworth, "Having of Wonderful Ideas," 224.

17. Duckworth, 222.

18. Nel Noddings, *The Challenge to Care in Schools: An Alternative Approach to Education* (New York: Teachers College Press, 1992), xi.

19. Nel Noddings, "The Caring Relation in Teaching," *Oxford Review of Education* 38, no. 6 (December 2012): 772. Italics in the original.

20. Noddings, *Challenge to Care*, xii.

21. Mitchel Resnick et al., "Scratch: Programming for All," *Communications of the ACM* 52, no. 11 (November 2009): 65.

22. Mitchel Resnick, *Lifelong Kindergarten: Cultivating Creativity through Projects, Passion, Peers, and Play* (Cambridge, MA: MIT Press, 2017), 168.

23. Resnick, *Lifelong Kindergarten*, 64.

24. Resnick, 140.

25. Mizuko Ito et al., *Hanging Out, Messing Around, and Geeking Out: Kids Living and Learning with New Media*, Tenth Anniversary ed. (Cambridge, MA: MIT Press, [2009] 2019), 245–246.

26. Ito et al., *Hanging Out*, 290.

27. Ito et al., 23.

28. Anthony Giddens, *The Constitution of Society: Outline of the Theory of Structuration* (Berkeley: University of California Press, 1984), 42.

29. Giddens, *Constitution of Society*, 53.

30. Giddens, 64.

31. Jean Lave and Etienne Wenger, *Situated Learning: Legitimate Peripheral Participation* (Cambridge, UK: Cambridge University Press, 1991), 93. Italics in the original.

32. Lave and Wenger, *Situated Learning*, 109. Italics in the original.

33. Lave and Wenger, 37. Italics in the original.

34. Jeanne Bamberger, Eleanor Duckworth, and Magdalene Lampert, *An Experiment in Teacher Development: Final Report* (Washington, DC: National Institute of Education, 1981), 21. Underscore in the original.

35. Bamberger, Duckworth, and Lampert, *Experiment in Teacher Development*, 22.

36. Jeanne Bamberger, Eleanor Duckworth, and Magdalene Lampert, *Analysis of Data from an Experiment in Teacher Development* (Washington, DC: National Institute of Education, 1982), 3. Underscore in the original.

37. bell hooks, *Teaching to Transgress: Education as the Practice of Freedom* (New York: Routledge, 1994), 8.

38. hooks, *Teaching to Transgress*, 8. Italics in the original.

39. hooks, 7.

40. hooks, 7.

41. John Dewey, *The School and Society* (Chicago: University of Chicago Press, 1900), 30–31.

42. Dewey, *School and Society*, 21.

43. Mihaly Csikszentmihalyi, *Creativity: Flow and the Psychology of Discovery and Invention* (New York: Harper Collins, 1996), 12.

44. Csikszentmihalyi, *Creativity*, 112.

45. Csikszentmihalyi, 66.

46. Donald Schön, *The Reflective Practitioner: How Professionals Think in Action* (New York: Basic Books, 1983).

47. Schön, *Reflective Practitioner*, 50.

48. Schön, 145.

49. Lev S. Vygotsky, *Mind in Society: The Development of Higher Psychological Processes* (Cambridge, MA: Harvard University Press, 1978), 86.

50. Vygotsky, *Mind in Society*, 91.

51. Audre Lorde, "There Is No Hierarchy of Oppressions," *Interracial Books for Children Bulletin* 14, nos. 3–4 (1983): 9.

52. Audre Lorde, "The Transformation of Silence into Language and Action," in *Sister Outsider: Essays and Speeches* (New York: Crossing Press, 1984), 42.

53. Lorde, "Transformation of Silence," 44.

54. Freire, *Pedagogy of Freedom*, 46–47.

55. Freire, 37–38.

56. Friedrich Froebel, *Education by Development* (New York: Appleton and Company, 1899), 59.

57. Friedrich Froebel, *Pedagogics of the Kindergarten* (New York: Appleton and Company, 1895), 61. Italics in the original.

58. Froebel, *Pedagogics of the Kindergarten*, 61.

59. Ivan Illich, *Deschooling Society* (New York: Harper & Row, 1970), 22.

60. Illich, *Deschooling*, 75.

61. Illich, xix.

62. Illich, 52.

63. Illich, 40.

64. Carol Dweck, *Self-Theories: Their Role in Motivation, Personality, and Development* (New York: Routledge, 2000), 27.

65. Dweck, *Self-Theories*, 17.

66. Jacques Rancière, *The Ignorant Schoolmaster: Five Lessons in Intellectual Emancipation* (Stanford, CA: Stanford University Press, 1991), 15.

67. Rancière, *Ignorant Schoolmaster*, 23.

68. Rancière, 66–67.

69. David Hawkins, *The Informed Vision* (New York: Algora Publishing, 2002), 51.

70. Hawkins, *Informed Vision*, 55.

71. Hawkins, 51–52.

72. Hawkins, 51.

73. Ursula Franklin, *The Real World of Technology*, rev. ed. (Toronto: Anansi, 1999), 20–21.

74. Seymour Papert, *Mindstorms*, 23.

75. Papert, *Mindstorms*, 115.

76. Papert, 114.

77. John Dewey, *Experience and Education* (New York: Kappa Delta Pi, 1938), 48.

78. Dewey, *Experience and Education*, 26.

79. Dewey, 49.

80. Sherry Turkle and Seymour Papert, "Epistemological Pluralism: Styles and Voices within the Computer Culture," *Signs: Journal of Women in Culture and Society* 16, no. 1 (Autumn 1990): 129.

81. Turkle and Papert, "Epistemological Pluralism," 135.

82. Ray McDermott and Hervé Varenne, "Culture *as* Disability," *Anthropology & Education Quarterly* 26, no. 3 (September 1995): 331–332.

83. McDermott and Varenne, "Culture *as* Disability," 326.

84. Barbara Rogoff, *Apprenticeship in Thinking: Cognitive Development in Social Context* (New York: Oxford University Press, 1990), ix.

85. Rogoff, *Apprenticeship in Thinking*, viii.

86. Rogoff, 39.

87. The book was *Liz Lerman's Critical Response Process* by Liz Lerman and John Borstel.

88. Richard Ryan and Edward Deci, "Self-Determination Theory and the Facilitation of Intrinsic Motivation, Social Development, and Well-Being," *American Psychologist* 55, no. 1 (January 2000): 68.

89. Ryan and Deci, "Self-Determination Theory," 74.

90. Postman and Weingartner, *Teaching as a Subversive Activity*, xiii.

91. Postman and Weingartner, 33. Italics in the original.

92. Gloria Ladson-Billings, *Culturally Relevant Pedagogy: Asking a Different Question* (New York: Teachers College Press, 2021), 153.

93. Gloria Ladson-Billings, "Toward a Theory of Culturally Relevant Pedagogy," *American Educational Research Journal* 32, no. 3 (Fall 1995): 480.

94. Rogers, *Freedom to Learn*, 5.

95. Rogers, 3. Italics in the original.

96. Rogers, 9. Italics in the original.

97. Rogers, 74. Italics in the original.

98. Henry Giroux, *Teachers as Intellectuals: Toward a Critical Pedagogy of Learning* (New York: Bergin & Garvey, 1988), 8.

99. Giroux, *Teachers as Intellectuals*, 3–4.

100. Giroux, 10.

101. Stuart Hall, "Encoding/Decoding," in *Media Studies: A Reader*, ed. Paul Marris and Sue Thornham (New York: Bergin & Garvey, 2000), 60.

102. Hall, "Encoding/Decoding," 58.

103. Lucy McCormick Calkins, *Lessons from a Child: On the Teaching and Learning of Writing* (Portsmouth, NH: Heinemann, 1983), 142.

104. Calkins, *Lessons from a Child*, 138.

105. Calkins, 131.

106. Lee Shulman, *The Wisdom of Practice: Essays on Teaching, Learning, and Learning to Teach* (San Francisco: Jossey-Bass, 2004), 517.

107. Shulman, *Wisdom of Practice*, 518.

108. Sherry Turkle, *Alone Together: Why We Expect More from Technology and Less from Each Other* (New York: Basic Books, 2011), 288.

109. Turkle, *Alone Together*, 263.

110. Jean Piaget, *The Child's Conception of the World* (Lanham, MD: Rowman & Littlefield, 2007), 6–7.

111. Eleanor Duckworth, "Piaget Rediscovered," *The Arithmetic Teacher* 11, no. 7 (November 1964): 499.

112. Project Zero and Reggio Children, *Making Learning Visible: Children as Individual and Group Learners* (Reggio Emilia, Italy: Reggio Children, 2001), 83.

113. Project Zero and Reggio Children, *Making Learning Visible*, 81.

114. Project Zero and Reggio Children, 81.

INDEX

This index consists of three parts: a listing of the *teachers* who participated in our research study and whose classrooms are featured in the book, a listing of the *theorists and texts* whose ideas motivated this work and deepened our understandings of these wonderful classrooms, and a listing of important *topics* from the book.

Teachers

Theorists and Texts

Topics

Publisher contact:
The MIT Press
Massachusetts Institute of Technology
77 Massachusetts Avenue, Cambridge, MA 02139
mitpress.mit.edu

EU Authorised Representative:
Easy Access System Europe, Mustamäe tee 50,
10621 Tallinn, Estonia
gpsr.requests@easproject.com

Printed by Integrated Books International,
United States of America